TIMELY WORDS

דבר בעתו
Timely Words

—∞—

Holiday Insights Throughout the Year

Moshe Sokolow

KODESH PRESS

TIMELY WORDS
Holiday Insights Throughout the Year
© Moshe Sokolow 2022

Hardcover ISBN: 978-1-947857-86-5
Paperback ISBN: 978-1-947857-87-2

All rights reserved. Except for brief quotations in printed reviews, no part of this publication may be reproduced, stored in a retrieval system, or transmitted in any form or by any means (printed, written, photocopied, visual electronic, audio, or otherwise) without the prior permission of the publisher.

PUBLISHED AND DISTRIBUTED EXCLUSIVELY BY
Kodesh Press LLC
New York, NY
www.kodeshpress.com
kodeshpress@gmail.com

Set in Arno Pro by Raphaël Freeman MISTD, Renana Typesetting
Printed in the United States of America

Timely Words

Fall: Hayamim Hanora'im: Rosh Hashanah, Yom Kippur

Warning: This *Shi'ur* May Contain Nuts	5
Prayer and Parnasah: What to Ask for on Rosh Hashanah	11
Whose Akeidah was it Anyhow? Comparative Jewish and Muslim Scriptural Exegesis	19
BeRosh Hashanah Yikateivun: Angels Dancing on a Silicon Chip	25
Teshuvah, Tefillah, uTzedakah: Does What We Say Mean What We Think?	43
Shalom Aleikhem Mal'akhei Rachamim: When Yom Kippur Falls on Shabbat	49

Winter: Thanksgiving, Hanukah, Tu BiShevat

Thanksgiving: A Heimische Holiday after All	57
VeTein Tal UMatar LiVerakhah: Who Sanctified the 5th of December? Insights into the Interplay between Calendar and Liturgy	61
VeHeikhan Tzivvanu: Are Hanukkah Lights a Torah Prescription?	73
Waging War on Shabbat: The Legacy of the Hashmonaim	83
"Twas the Night before Christmas": A Look at Nittel Nacht	91

Tu BiShevat: From New Year to Arbor Day	95

Spring: Purim, Pesach, Yom Ha'Atzma'ut, Yom Yerushalayim

Purim and the Story of Joseph: Design or Coincidence?	103
The *Korban Pesach* and the Repudiation of Idolatry	109
Don't Sit under the Apple Tree: *Charoset* and *Etrogim*	117
Shir HaShirim Inside and Out: The Perspective of Rav Kook	125
Flowering Trees, Flourishing Redemption: The Prayer for the Welfare of the State of Israel	135
In Pursuit of Peace	141
Sifra VeSaifa: Should Yeshiva Students do Military Service?	147
Land Purchases in Eretz Yisrael	167
Jerusalem and the Temple Mount in Jewish History	167

Summer: Shavu'ot, Tish'a BeAv

The *Azharot* of Rabbi Sa'adiah Gaon: An Exercise in *Ta'amei HaMitzvot*	179
Wake up and Smell the Torah	185
The World in Suspended Animation: *Matan Torah*	189
Sheyibaneh Beit HaMikdash: Rav Kook, Rabbi Hayyim Hirschensohn, and Theodor Herzl on Rebuilding the Temple	195

Prologue

The twenty-five units that follow were composed over an equal number of years, first under the auspices of the Torah Education and Culture Department of the World Zionist Organization, then under the rubric of the Torah Education Network (later The Association of Modern Orthodox Day Schools and Yeshiva High Schools), and, finally, in my capacity as a professor at the Azrieli Graduate School of Yeshiva University. They represent an ongoing concern with "pedagogical content knowledge" in *limmudei kodesh* and with maintaining the centrality of the Land of Israel and the People of Israel in learning the Torah of Israel.

This also accounts for the multidisciplinary nature of most of the selections. Even if they have a singular disciplinary point of departure – a biblical text, historical event, life-cycle issue, philosophical or ideological moral – they were constructed with the intent to make them easy to utilize in the widest variety of curricular and disciplinary settings, including schools, synagogues, private study; i.e., wherever Torah is valued. I was guided in this respect by the *Mekhilta* cited by Rashi in his opening remarks to *Mishpatim* (Exodus 21):

> God said to Moses: Do not imagine that you can just recite to them the law two or three times until they have it word perfect, but need not bother yourself to have them understand the rationales of the matters and their explanations. Therefore

the verse states: "[These are the statutes] that you shall place before them," as a table that is set before a person (*keshulchan he'arukh*) and ready to eat thereof.

Hence, the book is organized according to the Jewish calendar year, commencing, in the fall, with the Yamim HaNora'im (Days of Awe), continuing through the winter with Hanukkah, the spring with Purim and Pesach, and concluding in the summer with Shavu'ot and Tish'a b'Av. These lessons can also be incorporated into a range of subject matter (Tanakh, Talmud, Jewish history, Jewish philosophy) or interspersed among such special occasions as days of celebration or remembrance.

At first glance, some of the essays may appear unconnected to the seasons to which they are assigned; upon closer inspection, however, the link shall be obvious. The opening chapter, "This Shi'ur May Contain Nuts," relates to the custom of not eating nuts on Rosh Hashanah, the Akeidah is read on the second day of that holiday, and "Angels Dancing on a Silicon Chip" is a somewhat humorous attempt to bring God's inscribing our fate into the age of computers. "Waging War on Shabbat" is subtitled "The Legacy of the Hashmonaim," whose victory over the Greeks we commemorate on Hanukkah. "Flowering Trees, Flourishing Redemption" is in honor of Yom Ha'Atzma'ut, Israel's Independence Day, as are the chapters on Hesder (military service for yeshiva students), and "The Pursuit of Peace." "Wake Up and Smell the Torah" marks the custom of studying Torah throughout the night (*tikun*) of Shavu'ot, and the final chapter, "Rebuilding the Temple," is apropos of the traditional assertion that Tish'a b'Av marks our incipient redemption.

Technicalities:

All translations are my own unless noted otherwise. The names of biblical books and characters are given in their accepted English forms (Moses, Samuel), but names of post-biblical personalities are rendered according to their modern Hebrew pronunciation (Moshe, Shemu'el). All talmudic references are to the Babylonian Talmud unless otherwise noted.

Acknowledgements:

I would be remiss if I did not express my gratitude to the late Hanokh Achiman who, as director of the wzo Torah Education Department, originally inspired this project; to Rabbi Robert Hirt who, as the driving force behind the Torah Education Network, nurtured its continuation; and to Dr. David Schnall and Dr. Rona Novick who, as deans of the Azrieli Graduate School of Jewish Education, supported its most recent iteration.

Dedication:

I dedicate this book to the generations fore and aft: my parents, Joseph and Hannah Sokolow, and in-laws, Sol and Roslyn Sussman, all of blessed memory; my wife, Judy, whose insights and good taste have, again, shepherded this book through its development; our children, Shalom and his wife Sharon; and our grandchildren, Naomi, Rafi, and Daniel.

לולי תורתך שעשעי, אז אבדתי בעניי.

Moshe Sokolow
May 2022
Iyar 5782

Warning: This Shi'ur May Contain Nuts
Symbolic Foods on Rosh Hashanah

Preface
The prohibition against eating nuts on Rosh Hashanah is well known and its observance is widespread. The reason behind the prohibition, however, is somewhat obscure. We shall investigate its sources, examine the ostensible reasons, and, in the process, propose one that may be more persuasive than those recorded in the sources.

SOURCES ON NUTS

R. Moses Isserles (Rema; 1520–1572), on the authority of R. Jacob Moelin (Maharil; 1365–1427), provided two reasons for the prohibition:

> Those who exercise caution (*hamedakdekim*) refrain from eating nuts, because nut (*egoz*) in alphanumerics (*gematriya*) equals sin (*cheit'*). Moreover, they cause much phlegm and mucous and thereby interfere with prayer. (*Orach Chayyim* 583:2)

R. Mordechai Yaffe (*Levush*; 1530–1612), the Rema's student, appealed to the first reason: "In other words, one should not consume a sin on Rosh Hashanah, the day on which we are judged on account of our sins" (ad. loc.).

R. Abraham Gombiner (*Magen Avraham*; 1633–1683), however, drew upon the alternative: "I have heard that a large [nut] is called *egoz* while a small one is called *luz*, [a distinction] recorded in *Shir ha-Shirim Rabbah*. According to the second reason, however, both are forbidden" (ad. loc.). In other words, if the reason for the prohibition is the numerical symmetry between *egoz* and *chet'*, then *luz*, which is unequal, should be permissible. If the reason, however, is the production of phlegm, any nut is problematic, size notwithstanding.

The Specifics

If nuts interfere with prayer, why are they not forbidden year-round? R. Joseph ben Meir Te'omim (*Pri Megadim*; 1727–1793) explained: "On Rosh Hashanah, we are required to be unusually noiseless and intent on the recitation of the emissary of the congregation (*shali'ach tzibbur*)" (cited by *Eshel Avraham* 583:4).

Tracing these remarks back to their source in R. Jacob Moelin (Maharil; 1365–1427) we can see that the original concern was with nuts' potential effect on the sounding of the shofar.

> All people should be cautious not to expectorate during the sounding of the shofar...in order to hear the entire sound without even the slightest interruption.... Therefore, anything that causes phlegm or mucous should not be eaten on Rosh Hashanah, for which reason there are those who are careful not to eat nuts on Rosh Hashanah before shofar blowing because it increases phlegm. (Maharil: *Minhagim, Shofar* 2)

While Maharil is the earliest source cited, it is implicit in his text that the custom preceded him ("for which reason there are those who are careful"). Indeed, one would be entitled to draw the conclusion that the prohibition itself harkened back to an earlier era, while the reason or reasons had been lost or overlooked in the passage of time.

Acalculia

Famously, simple arithmetic throws this prescribed caution to the proverbial winds: The value of *egoz* in *gematriya* is 17, while that of *cheit'* is 18! Moreover, it may be noted that 17 is also the value of the Hebrew word *tov*, "good." Indeed, there is an attestation to this perplexity in a most unlikely place: the printed commentary of Rashi to Isaiah 11:1, "And a shoot shall emerge from the trunk of Jesse…":

> The copyist said: In the autumn of my days, I queried several sages regarding that which my grandfather the Rema had written about the numerical value of nut equaling sin: Is it not also equal to good?

While this comment is patently not Rashi's own, the master did have something to say about nuts elsewhere:

> Why is Israel likened to nuts? Just as a nut looks like wood and its inside is concealed, but once broken open it is found to be filled with edible contents, so is Israel possessed of modest and humble deeds and its sages are unseen and unheralded. If one examines it, however, one discovers it is filled with wisdom. Other homilies include: Just as a nut can fall into the mud without dirtying its contents, so can Israel be exiled among the Gentiles and beaten without sullying their deeds (on Song of Songs 6:11).

OTHER SIGNS, SYMBOLS, AND OMENS

Whenever one deals with the festive menu for Rosh Hashanah, one is bound to encounter the concept of signs or symbols (*simanim*) first introduced by the Amora Abbaye:

> Now that we have determined that symbols have significance, one should always make it a practice to view[1] on Rosh Hashanah

---
1. Other citations (*Keritot* 6a) read: "eat."

qara (squash), *rubya* (beans), *karti* (leeks), *silka* (beets), and *tamri* (dates) (*Horiyot* 12a).

Pursuant to the significance attached to signs and symbols, a novel suggestion, also based on a pun, speculated that the prohibition against nuts originated on account of its German (or Yiddish) translation "nus," which sounds like Hebrew *la-nus,* "to flee," and was regarded as a bad omen.[2] Lest this appear extreme or jejune, let us note that fish suffered a similar fate. According to Hida (Hayyim Yosef David Azulay, 1724–1806):

> Abu Dirham[3] (Spain, 14th century) wrote that one should eat fish [on Rosh Hashanah]. R. Shimon ben Tzemah Duran (Rashbatz; 1361–1444) wrote that one should be cautious on account of its name [*dag*], because we have found in Scripture the word "anxiety" (*da'ag*; Nehemiah 13:16) (*Birkei Yosef; Orach Chayyim* 583).[4]

Honey and Sweets on Rosh Hashanah

The association of Rosh Hashanah and sweets is traced back by R. Eliezer ben Yoel ha-Levi (Ravyah; 1140–1225) to one of the earliest celebrations of the New Year after the restoration following the Babylonian exile:

> In the Book of Ezra[5] we find that they wept upon their return from captivity. Ezra told them: "Be not anxious, for today is

---

2. Mordekhai Manovitz: "Nuts on Rosh Hashanah," Bar Ilan University Pararshat Hashavua Study Center, September, 2006: http://www.biu.ac.il/JH/Parasha/eng/rosh/man.html.
3. Usually, but erroneously, pronounced Abudraham.
4. The historian Shaul Stampfer, collecting Eastern European Jewish customs pertaining to food, was informed (orally) that "there is a Hasidic custom not to eat fish on the second day of Rosh Hashanah because fish eat the sins thrown into the water during the *Tashlikh* ceremony" (performed on the first day).
5. The reference is to Nehemiah 8:10. In talmudic and medieval times, however, the books of Ezra and Nehemiah were considered as one book.

sacred to God." And he said: "Eat rich foods and drink sweets" so that it will be a good, rich, and sweet year... (Rosh Hashanah #537).

Maharil explained:

> The reason for eating sweet stuff is that God should grant us a good and sweet year. In Ashkenaz people customarily eat a sweet apple in honey at the start of the meal, and recite: "We should be granted a good and sweet year." This is deduced from verses in Torah, Prophets, and Scriptures... (Several such verses are cited along with their homiletic interpretations.)

Maharil declared that no single reason is adequate because not one successfully explains why an apple is prefered when there are many types of sweet foods and, furthermore, not all apples are sweet. His answer is that this is an allusion to a specific field of apples – known to mystics – to which Isaac referred in saying to Jacob: "Behold, my son's scent is like that of the field that God blessed" (Genesis 27:27).[6]

LIFE AND DEATH

The alternative explanation alluded to in the preface and in the title of this chapter is an extreme allergic reaction called anaphylaxis. It is not unreasonable to assume that the the well-known association of nuts with shock and, in extreme cases, death due to asphyxiation, contributed to the custom of avoiding nuts on Rosh Hashanah, a day on which, most poignantly, the "Books of Life and Death" lie open before God. Indeed, a popular inability to understand why some people might die of mere exposure to nuts while most are able to ingest them with impunity may have inspired the intimation that sin is involved, expressed by the *gematriya* of *egoz=cheit'*.

---

6. As to that particular custom that is enshrined in the kindergarten ditty "Dip the *apple* in the honey... have a very sweet new year," see our remarks entitled: "Don't Sit under the Apple Tree," apropos of the holiday of Passover.

Prayer and Parnasah
What to Ask for on Rosh Hashanah

Prologue
Three propositions inform this chapter:

- One's livelihood (*parnasah*) for the coming year is determined on Rosh Hashanah.
- One's prayers on Rosh Hashanah can beneficially influence one's livelihood.
- God invites our prayers and our words of prayer influence Him, particularly in the matter of our livelihood.

Resolving a Contradiction
In Genesis 1:12, the Torah indicates that grass had begun to grow on day three of creation (*vatotzei ha'aretz deshe'*). In 2:5, however, it implies that there was no vegetation (*vekhol 'eisev hasadeh terem yitzmach*) – because there was no precipitation (*ki lo himtir*) – prior to the creation of man on day six (*ve'adam ayin la'avod et ha'adamah*).

R. Assi resolved this contradiction (*Chullin* 60b) by positing that between day three and day six the vegetation was kept poised just below the surface of the earth. When Adam came, he recited a prayer for rain and it broke through the surface. From this resolution, R.

Assi then infered a momentous theological postulate: "God craves (*mit'avveh*) the prayer[1] of the righteous."

Reducing this theological proposition to more existential terms, it places man – rather than the earth – at the focus of creation and indicates that God's principal purpose in creation was not the earth itself but earth-dwellers. Adam, the first human, was not intended to emerge upon the background of a completed and perfect world but to be co-opted into partnering with God in its completion and perfection. God, therefore, did not provide him merely with the opportunity or even just the incentive to pray for the rain that would complete creation; He positively craved his prayer, for without it, God's own plan and intent would have been frustrated.

The consequences of this realization are exceedingly far-reaching. As much as we are dependent upon God and His grace (*chesed*), so is He dependent upon our participation in His worldly enterprise. That would appear to give us considerable leverage to wield in our dealings with Him.

Some Thoughts About the Mutuality of Prayer

In Numbers 28:2, in regard to the "regular near-offerings" (*korban tamid*), God put us in charge of what He called: "My near-offering (*korbani*), My food (*lachmi*), My fire-offerings (*le'ishai*), My soothing savor (*rei'ach nichochi*)."[2] This permits – or, perhaps, even mandates – the following syllogism:

---

1. This is an apt moment to point out the inadequacy of the word "prayer" as the translation of *tefillah*. The etymology of "prayer" in English yields "petition" or "request," for which the Hebrew is *bakkashah*, a component of *tefillah* but not completely identical with it. The root of *tefillah*, p-l-l, however, indicates judgment, and in its reflexive form, *lehitpallel*, means self-judgment or introspection. For the purpose of clarity, we shall continue our use of "prayer." See the section on "Etymology" at the beginning of the next chapter.

2. Translations following Everett Fox: *The Five Books of Moses* (Schocken). Since the root of *korban* is k-r-b, I prefer his more literal "near-offering" to the customary "sacrifice," whose etymology derives it from the Latin for holy – for

1. Sacrifices are God's sustenance, so to speak, and He looks to us for His satisfaction.
2. Prayer is the substitute for sacrifices.
3. Therefore, God looks forward to our regular prayer just as He previously looked forward to our regular sacrifices.

Our prayer then, is decidedly not a one-sided affair in which we beseech God for unmerited divine assistance, favor, or grace. On the contrary, it is part of a pact, a covenant if you will, between parties who, however unequal in capacity, are nonetheless mutually dependent.[3]

The Connection Between Prayer and Parnasah

Rabbi Naftali Tzvi Yehudah Berlin (Netziv; 1817–1893) explained that according to the Sages, the word *si'ach* (in Gen. 2:5, a bush) also denotes prayer (*Avodah Zarah* 7b).

> This is the difference between all *mitzvot* of the Torah and sacrifices or prayer. All the other *mitzvot* and forms of worship either have their rewards withheld until the world to come, or their benefits are reaped directly in this world – in wealth and honor and the like, a quid pro quo (*midah keneged midah*).
>
> Sacrifices and prayer, on the other hand, are essentially [performed] in order to promote livelihood. To wit: "[Why is the altar called] *mizbe'ach*? Because it is *meizin* [provides sustenance]" (*Ketubot* 10b).
>
> Established prayer [*tefillah kevu'ah*] is similarly referred to as "temporal life" (*chayyei sha'ah*) and all the blessings over pleasure [*birkhot ha-nehenin*] are likewise meant to bless the abundance of that species.

---

which we would expect, in Hebrew, a form of the verb *k-d-sh*. For the same purpose of clarity (cited in the previous note), we will continue to use "sacrifice."

3. Rabbi Joseph B. Soloveitchik similarly characterized prayer as a "dialogue" between man and God. See M. Sokolow: *Reading the Rav* (NY: Kodesh, 2018), *passim*.

We note in *Berakhot* (35a) that taking pleasure in this world without reciting a blessing is comparable to stealing from God and the community of Israel, to wit: "One who steals from his father or mother saying, 'It is no crime,' is akin to a man of destruction" (Proverbs 28:24), such as Jeroboam son of Nebat who destroyed [the relationship] between Israel and its heavenly Father.

The meaning behind this is as follows: The blessings over pleasure cause the abundance of that species and whoever withholds these blessings is stealing from God, Who wishes to provide the abundance, and from the community of Israel, which is in need of it. He is akin to Jeroboam who [by erecting the golden calves] prevented Israel from bringing the sacrifices that stimulate blessing (*Ha'ameik Davar* to Genesis 2:5).

Complementarity and *Kavvanah*

The concept that our prayer and God's satisfaction are symbiotic appears to be the basis for a talmudic prescription for the proper direction toward which prayer should be addressed:

> One standing in the Diaspora should direct his heart [*yekhavven libbo*] towards the Land of Israel... In the Land of Israel, towards Jerusalem... In Jerusalem, towards the Temple... In the Temple, towards the Holy of Holies... In the Holy of Holies, towards the *kapporet*... One standing behind the *kapporet* should pretend he is before it. The result is that one standing in the east – faces west; west – faces east; south – faces north; and north – faces south. The result is that all Israel direct their hearts towards one place (*Berakhot* 30a).

Why did the *kapporet*[4] become the narrowest focus of the prayers of all Israel? Two verses provide the answer:

---

4. The so-called "mercy seat," which was a piece of pure gold that rested atop the Holy Ark. Cf., e.g., Exodus 25:17 ff.

1. "I shall meet with you there, and I shall speak with you from above the *kapporet*, from between the two cherubs [*keruvim*], which are atop the Ark of the Covenant…" (Exodus 25:22).
2. "When Moses entered the tent of meeting to speak with Him, he heard the voice discoursing with him from above the *kapporet* atop the Ark of the Covenant, from between the two cherubs…" (Numbers 7:89).

Because it was from the *kapporet* that the voice of God emanated in addressing Moses, it is to that selfsame *kapporet* that Israel addresses its hearts in prayer.

Kofer, Kapporet, Kapparah, and Yom Ha-Kippurim

The root *k-p-r* is a homonymous one in the Bible, denoting several, albeit related, but different things. The specific aspect with which we will deal here is the one signifying the noun "pitch" (*kofer*), and the verb "to coat [with pitch]" (see Gen. 6:14: "coat it [Noah's ark], inside and out, with pitch").

By metaphorical extension, *k-p-r* also means "to cover over, pacify, or propitiate" (see Gen. 32:21: "I shall pacify/propitiate him"),[5] whence we derive the noun "ransom, or price of life" (Exodus 21:30: "Should ransom be designated, he shall pay the price (*kofer*) of his life").

Coming closer to our purpose – both textually and contextually – is Moses's statement in Exodus 32:30: "You have erred/sinned grievously… perhaps I can cover over your error/sin." Rashi, appreciating both the literal and metaphorical usage of *k-p-r*, commented: "I shall place a coating (*kofer*), or filling (*setimah*), at the site of the sin, to keep you disengaged from it." *Kofer*, in these terms, is the stuff with which we fill in the chinks that sin causes to develop in our spiritual armor.

When do we apply this *kofer*? On the "Day of Atonement," a word that has a decidedly delicious derivation from the Middle English "at one," meaning "agreed." Yom ha-Kippurim is – literally as well as

---

5. See in detail, "'Face to Face': An Exercise in Theme Words," below.

homiletically – a "Day of At-one-ment." Recasting Rashi's metaphor, it is a "Day of Bonding." By closing the apertures of the soul and sealing them against erosion due to the friction of error and sin, man becomes one with God.

As noted, the *kapporet* was a slab of pure gold that reposed atop the Ark of the Covenant in the Tabernacle (Exodus 25:17 ff.), fitted to its outer dimensions. Its relationship to the usages of *k-p-r*, which we have already demonstrated, is illustrated by its translation, in older English versions (based upon the Septuagint and the Vulgate), as "mercy seat," deriving its name from the notion of propitiation. In order to secure *kapparah* for the Jewish people on Yom ha-Kippurim, Aaron is instructed to sprinkle the blood of the sin-offering "on and before the *kapporet*" (Lev. 16:15–16).

Conclusion

Just as Moses, at Sinai, stood in the cleft of the rock clutching the tablets of the Law, as God, in a cloud, first revealed His attributes of compassion and grace, so was Aaron instructed to seek atonement for the Jewish people by replicating the circumstances of Moses's revelation. The *kapporet* replaced the "cleft of the rock" in which Moses stood, and the "cloud of incense" (*'anan ha-ketoret*) replicated the "thickness of the cloud" (*'av he-'anan*) from within which God spoke.

We, who have neither the cleft of the rock nor the *kapporet*, and who can produce neither genuine clouds nor those of incense, must rely upon the order of prayer of Rosh Hashanah, invoking the thirteen attributes of grace and compassion, and the *selichot*, a significant feature of the liturgical order of Yom Kippur, invoking God's juridical capacity to pardon and atone.

Finally, it was only after Adam sinned and was banished from Eden that he was assigned the task "to work the earth whence he was taken" (Genesis 3:23). Assumedly, this is the juncture at which he prayed, as explained above by the Netziv. Additional significance, then, attaches to the fact that immediately thereafter God set up two *keruvim* (cherubs) "to guard the way to the tree of life" (3:24). These were, arguably, the same two *keruvim* that crowned the *kapporet*, from between whose outstretched wings God spoke, and towards which we direct our prayers.⁶

---

6. Note that in the latter verse in Genesis, the path to the *'eitz ha-chayyim* is guarded by *lahav ha-cherev ha-mithappekhet*, translated, variously, as "a flaming sword that turned each way" (King James Version), or "the fiery revolving sword" (New American Bible). I would suggest that it is better understood as a rotating sword. Since ordinary swords are sharpened on only one side and blunt on the other, anyone attempting to pass by such a sword could do so fully fifty percent of the time – providing he knew the timing of its rotation. Perhaps this is in recognition of the fact that Torah, too, can be used either constructively, in which case it becomes an "elixir of life" (*sam ha-chayyim*), or it can be abused, in which case it becomes a "lethal potion" (*sam ha-mavet*). The ability to distinguish between the two would facilitate the synchronization with the rotating sword and, ultimately, reopen the way to the *'eitz ha-chayyim* – a biblical euphemism for the Torah (Proverbs 3:18).

Whose Akeidah Was It Anyhow?
Comparative Scriptural Exegesis

Preface

On July 19–23, 2021 (1442 of the Muslim era),[1] Muslims the world over celebrated *'Id al-Adha*, the Festival of the Sacrifice. Also known as the great festival (*'id al-kabir*, in contrast to *'id al-fitr*, the festival that breaks the fast of Ramadan, which is also known as *'id al-saghir*, the lesser festival), it commemorates Abraham's preparedness to demonstrate his love of God through the sacrifice of his son. The parallels with the biblical episode of the Binding of Isaac (*'akeidah*) are unmistakable.

But the Qur'an does not explicitly name the son Abraham intended to sacrifice. While most Muslims assume that it was Ishmael, it is noteworthy that this was not the unanimous opinion of early Muslims and Qur'anic scholars. Indeed, a tabulation of authoritative medieval Qur'anic commentaries yields the remarkable distribution of 133 scholars favoring Ishmael, with fully 130 others favoring Isaac.[2] By reviewing the Qur'anic text in question and noting what motivated the commentators in their interpretations, we can learn a good deal about Islam and its relationship to biblical and rabbinic Jewish tradition.

---

1. See our discussion of the Muslim calendar and chronology below in the chapter entitled "Who Sanctified the 5th of December?"
2. Bernard Firestone, *Journeys in Holy Lands* (Albany: SUNY, 1990), 135.

Introducing the Qur'an

The Qur'an (alt: Koran, Arabic for "recitation"; related, philologically, to *Mikra'*, the talmudic and medieval Hebrew word for "Scripture") is arranged in size order. With the exception of the first chapter, which is considered an introduction and proclamation of faith,[3] the second chapter is the longest and the last chapter (#114) is the shortest. Each chapter is also assigned to either "Mecca" or "Medinah," the two principal cities of Islam, depending on where it is believed to have been revealed to Muhammad. The Qur'an is also divided into thirty sections, corresponding to the thirty days of the month of Ramadan, during which some Muslims have the custom of reading through the entire book. The chapter (*surah*) that features the story of the sacrifice is number 37, entitled "The Ranks," and designated "Meccan."

After introducing Noah (Nuch) and describing his righteousness, the chapter moves on to Abraham (Ibrahim) and his miraculous rescue from the fire into which he was thrown due to his belief in God – an account found in the Jewish Aggadah as well. It is noteworthy that the Qur'an bestows upon Abraham the epithet of *al-Khalil*, "the friend (of God)," which is also the Arabic name for Abraham's city, Hebron, whose Hebrew name, *Chevron*, also implies friendship (*chaver*).

The 'Akeidah

The parallel "Akeidah" story follows thereupon (vs. 100 ff.). We present it here in a close paraphrase, with exact quotations marked.

> Abraham prayed to God to grant him righteous progeny. God told him that he would have a gentle son. When the boy began to run about with him, Abraham told his son that he saw himself, in a dream, slaughtering him. The son replied: "Do what you are commanded. God willing, I will be steadfast." When both were ready to submit to God's will and Abraham had

---

3. It is entitled "*al-Faticha*," related to the Hebrew word *petichah*, an opening.

cast his son down upon his face, God called to him saying: "Abraham. You have indeed fulfilled the vision... This was surely a clear trial." God then ransomed the boy with "a great sacrifice."

The chapter continues with the tidings about the birth of Isaac (and also mentions Moses, Aaron, Elijah, Lot, and Jonah).

But which son was it? On the one hand, the Qur'an does not explicitly name the son whom Abraham prepared to sacrifice. On the other hand, however, its subsequent reference to the tidings about the birth of Isaac would seem to imply that the son mentioned previously in the chapter was not Isaac – but Ishmael. Indeed, that is the opinion of most commentators, as we noted at the outset. Of greater interest and significance, however, is the minority opinion. To view both opinions, we turn to one of the foremost commentators on the Qur'an, Abu Ja'afar Muhammad al-Tabari (d. 923).

According to Tabari, an exponent of the method of scriptural interpretation that biblical commentators would call simple and straightforward (*peshat*), every reference in the Qur'an to tidings about a child (such as Q 11:71) refers to Isaac. In that case, Abraham's prayer for a child in chapter 37 (see above) must also refer to Isaac and therefore Isaac is the subject of the sacrificial story, too.

In spite of his own preference for Isaac, Tabari dutifully cited the arguments for Ishmael: Since God, by commanding the sacrifice, could not have abrogated His promise to Abraham that Isaac, himself, would have a son (also Q 11:71), the intended sacrifice must have been Ishmael. (The identical theme – the ostensible abrogation of God's promise – is struck by the Midrash in *Genesis Rabbah* 56, albeit with a very different solution.)[4]

---

4. Since the completion of this book, I have published an essay entitled: "How (Not) to Teach the Akeidah," Megadim 60 (2021), 9–20, in which this Midrash features prominently.

Muslims, Jewish Converts, and Folklore

The early Muslims knew that stories about Abraham (recognized as the progenitor of the Arabs via Ishmael) and Isaac had already been told in the Jewish Bible and had become part of Arabian Jewish folklore (known, in Arabic, as Isra'iliyat). In fact, Muhammad and his successors, the Caliphs, had several companions who were converts from Judaism. Some, like Ka'b al-Achbar,[5] had a profound impact on the early Muslims' understanding of the many Qur'anic references to biblical personalities and events.

Indeed, according to post-Qur'anic Islamic tradition (*hadith*), when the Caliph Umar (c. 640) was questioned on our subject, he summoned such a convert and asked him: "Which of his two sons was Abraham commanded to sacrifice?" The convert answered: "Ishmael, by God, O Prince of the Believers." While his reply was clearly intended to ingratiate himself with the Caliph, it is significant that his argument, which follows, attached to that sacrifice the very importance that Jewish tradition attaches to the *Akeidah*:

> The Jews know that, but they are envious of you, O Arabs, because it was your father [Ishmael] who was named in God's command and to whom God ascribed such merit for his steadfastness in obeying God's command. They reject that, and claim that it was Isaac, because Isaac was their father. (Tabari, *History*, vol. II, 88)

The "great sacrifice" that God allowed Abraham to substitute for his son is identified in some Muslim traditions as a ram (whose horns were once said to hang in the Ka'ba shrine in Mecca, see below) and in other traditions as a sheep. It is the forerunner of the annual sacrifice

---

5. *Achbar* is an Arabicized form of the title *chaver* (colleague) that the Talmud uses to designate a person knowledgeable in the abstruse laws of purity. Ka'b, then, was a learned Jew prior to his conversion and a likely source for Muslims of much information about Jews and Judaism. See "Jerusalem between Jews and Muslims," below.

that was celebrated during the *'Id al-Adha* festival that occurs during the twelfth (and final) month of the Muslim lunar calendar, *Dhu al-Hijja*.

The Ka'Aba and the Pilgrimage (Haj) to Mecca

Pilgrimage to Mecca (Arabic: *haj*, related to Hebrew *chag*, "festival") is one of the five "pillars" of Islam, and is incumbent upon every Muslim at least once in a lifetime. The preferred time for a pilgrimage is during the four months that commence with the twelfth month of the lunar year, Dhu al-Hijja.

The focus of the pilgrimage is the Ka'ba, which, according to the Qur'an (2:127), was built by Abraham and Ishmael. Today it is a somewhat cube-like, mostly black structure, occupying the center of an immense public square in Mecca and is usually surrounded by thousands upon thousands of pilgrims. Inside the structure, is a black rock – possibly a meteor[6] – which has occupied the site since pre-Islamic times. According to Muslim tradition, the stone, a gift from God, was originally white, but the touch of many sinners blackened it.

After bathing, pilgrims enter a state of purity (Arabic: *ihram*, related to the Hebrew: *cherem*), in which it is forbidden to engage in violence or sexual activity, and perform a ritual known as "standing before God" (*waqfa*), which takes place at the Mount of Mercy nine miles east of Mecca, at a site called Arafat. Dressed in white, the pilgrims perform seven circumambulations of the Ka'ba both at the beginning

---

6. Louis Ginzberg, in *Legends of the Jews* vol. v (Phila., 1913), 15, suggested that the name *'even ha-shetiyah* (the so-called "foundation stone" situated on the Temple Mount beneath the Holy of Holies) was originally *'even 'eishata* (fire-stone), reflecting a tradition that the stone was a meteor that fell to earth in Jerusalem during the time of the early prophets (cf. *Yoma* 5:2): "Later, however, *'even ha-sh'tiyah* was related to *sh'ti*, 'loom' (creation as a spinning out of skeins of the warp is a favorite image) or *sh'ti*, "foundation." If Ginzberg's theory about its extraterrestrial origin is correct, there is an obvious connection between the Foundation Rock and the Ka'ba in Mecca that may well have inspired the many traditions that speak of them in similar terms.

and conclusion of the ritual. This activity is reminiscent of either the seven circumambulations of Jericho prior to its collapse or the annual seven circumambulations of the altar (*hakkafot*) that were performed on Sukkot.

Another part of the pilgrimage ritual consists of casting stones at Satan at a place called Mina, near Mecca. While Maimonides, in a responsum, ruled that this is not an idolatrous practice *per se*, it is a vestige of a pagan practice condemned by the Talmud (*Sanhedrin* 60b), which stipulated that to cast a stone at Mercury is to worship it (*ha-zorek 'even le-markolis, zo hi 'avodatah*).

Sound Familiar?

Bathing, dressing in white, and doing something seven times are practices highly reminiscent of certain Jewish rituals – particularly those of Yom HaKippurim. Indeed, there is significant evidence that, of all the Jewish rituals with which Muhammad may have been acquainted, those of Yom HaKippurim made the greatest impression on him.

Indeed, this also relates to the five daily prayers in Islam. Some scholars have explained it as a compromise between the normative Jewish practice of three and a sectarian Jewish practice of seven (based on Psalms 119:164: "I have praised You seven times daily"). A more reasonable explanation connects it to Yom Kippur, the only day in the year on which the addition of the Ne'ilah service (to the four that are standard for Shabbat or Yom Tov) brings the number of prayers to five.

Angels Dancing on a Silicon Chip
Who Is in Charge of Heavenly Computing?*

Preface

It was not long after we brought home our first desktop computer that my wife speculated as to whether God had replaced the old-fashioned method of manually recording human fate – to which we make ample liturgical reference on the Days of Awe[1] – with a computer.

We shall endeavor to answer this question, albeit in a somewhat oblique fashion, by addressing a corollary: If God has indeed entered the cyber-age, which of his many ministering angels oversees the heavenly technology?

This chapter – written with a modicum of tongue in cheek – is divided into two parts. In the first, An Introduction to Jewish Angelology, I present an overview of angels in the classical Jewish literary tradition from the Bible through the twentieth century. Here, we encounter

---

* My thanks to Dr. Judy Cahn, educational technologist extraordinaire, for inspiration and assistance. For a survey of the role of technology in day school education, see *Jewish Educational Leadership* 9:1 (Fall, 2010).

1. E.g., בראש השנה ייכתבון, וביום צום כיפור יחתמון; "On Rosh Hashanah [our destiny] is inscribed and on the fast of [Yom] Kippur it is sealed," from which we derive the traditional New Year's greeting: כתיבה וחתימה טובה. Alternately, the insert in the closing blessing of the *Amidah*: וכתוב לחיים טובים כל בני בריתך; "inscribe all members of Your covenant for a good life."

scores of angels – anonymous and named – including several whose designated functions approximate the task we are addressing.

In the second part, Angels and Computing, we pose several alternative views of computer technology – from "mere" data processing, through retention and retrieval, to artificial intelligence – and relate those prospective functions to the angelic tasks to which they appear to bear the greatest affinity. Finally, we address the ostensibly fundamental dissonance between the widely variegated functioning of a computer – known as "multi-tasking" – and the rabbinic proposition that angels can fulfill only discrete tasks.

God and Computing: A Theological Preface

Anthropomorphism is the contemplation of God in human, corporeal, terms. Anthropopathism is the consideration of God through the prism of human emotions. In this essay, we ponder whether we need to introduce another theological category, "anthropocyberism" – imputing to God the current human preoccupation with computers and technology.

It has long been a part of Jewish literary tradition that every function in the universe is under the supervision of an angel. It is further understood that each function requires a separate agent, since "a single angel cannot perform two tasks."[2] How do we reconcile this folk-wisdom with the proposition that multi-tasking, "the apparent simultaneous performance of two or more tasks," is a quintessential, even indispensable, feature of computing?

---

2. *Bereishit Rabbah* 50:2. אין מלאך אחד עושה שתי שליחויות.

An Introduction to Jewish Angelology

A Philological Foreword

The English word "angel" derives from the classical Greek *angelos*, which means "messenger." Popular usage, however, tends to reserve its use for celestial creatures usually dressed in white, winged and haloed, and perhaps carrying a harp. The operative question is: When the word מלאך appears in a biblical text, does it refer to the mortal or the celestial variety of messenger? The operative answer is: It depends on the context.

Angels in the Bible

A. TORAH

The two *mal'akhim* who visited Lot (Genesis 19:1) appear to be of the celestial variety – since otherwise they would not have had the capacity to destroy Sodom – as were the *mal'akhim* envisioned by Jacob in his dream (Gen. 28:12). When we come, however, to the *mal'akhim* whom Jacob dispatched before him to Esau (Gen. 32:4), traditional opinion is divided between those, like Rashi, who saw them as celestial, and those, like Ibn Ezra and Radak, who emphasized that they were human. A useful rule of thumb to distinguish between these possibilities is that wherever the Aramaic version known as Targum Onkelos considers *mal'akhim* to be "angelic," it translates the word as *mal'akhaya*, whereas if it regards them as human, it uses *izgadin*, ordinary messengers.

A similar disagreement exists concerning the *'ish* who found Joseph in the field outside of Shechem and directed him to his brothers in Dothan (Gen. 37:15). Rashi identified him as the Angel Gabriel, while Ibn Ezra stipulated that he was only "an ordinary wayfarer." It is Nahmanides, however, who offered us a poignant insight into the rabbinic concept of angels, saying: "God summoned a guide [for Joseph] without his knowledge, in order that he may fall into [his brothers'] hands. This is what our Rabbis intended when they called such characters 'angels.'"[1] Finally, a *mal'akh* is mentioned by God as His deputy to lead Israel if God, in righteous indignation, were to leave them (Exodus 23:23; 32:34).

B. PROPHETS: EARLY AND LATER

An "angel" addressed Israel after the death of Joshua (Judges 2:1), one visited Gideon and charged him with his mission (6:11), and another one foretold the birth of Samson to his parents (13:3). Significantly, it is only when the last-mentioned angel ascended in the flame atop the altar that Manoah recognized his identity (13:20–21), implying that angels were able to assume a form that is indistinguishable from ordinary humans. Another "angel" was the intermediary for punishing the inhabitants of Jerusalem towards the close of the reign of King David (2 Samuel 24:16) and an "angel of God" slew 185,000 Assyrian soldiers who were besieging Jerusalem (2 Kings 19:35)

Angels made more regular appearances in the era of the Babylonian exile and the restoration of Zion. Zachariah had a frequent angelic interlocutor (המלאך הדובר בי 1:9, 13–14; 2:2,7; 4:1,4,5; et passim). Somewhat paradigmatic of this tendency is the fact that the last-named prophet in the Bible (who was a contemporary of Daniel and Zachariah) was actually named Malachi, Hebrew for "angel."

---

1. כי זִמֵּן לו הקב"ה מורה דרך שלא מדעתו להביאו בידם. ולזה נתכוונו רבותינו באמרם כי האישים האלה הם מלאכים .. See "Purim and Joseph," below.

C. KETUVIM

A brief glance at biblical poetry indicates that angel is used synonymously with slave or servant, as in Psalm 104:4: "Who makes the winds His angels and blazing light His servants,"[2] and Job 4:18: "He places no faith in his slaves and casts doubt upon his angels."[3] The Book of Daniel takes particular note of Gabriel in chapters 8–9 and of Michael in chapters 10 and 12.

Angels in the Apocrypha, Pseudepigrapha and Dead Sea Scrolls

Appearances by angels increase significantly in post-biblical Jewish literature. (It increased even more in the New Testament, but that is well outside our purview.) The Book of Tobit introduced Raphael, the angel of healing, and 2 Esdras introduced Uriel as Ezra's teacher. Both books – included in the Apocrypha – are presumed to have been composed in Hebrew. The book that names the most angels (more than 100), however, is 1 Enoch, which was composed in Greek. The Books of Maccabees report that angels assisted in the battles against the Greeks (2:11, 6–11; 3:6, 18–21; 4:4, 9–10).

The Dead Sea scroll "The War of the Sons of Light and Sons of Darkness" mentions four angels by name: Michael, Gabriel, Raphael, and Sariel (Chapter 9).

Angels in the Talmud and Midrash

It is in the Talmud and Midrash, however, that we find angelology fully developed. Here, we encounter angels who are assigned specific supervisory tasks:

- The angel in charge of conception is named "Night" (לילה)[4]

---

2. עֹשֶׂה מַלְאָכָיו רוּחוֹת מְשָׁרְתָיו אֵשׁ לֹהֵט
3. הֵן בַּעֲבָדָיו לֹא יַאֲמִין וּבְמַלְאָכָיו יָשִׂים תָּהֳלָה
4. BT *Niddah* (16b). See Job 3:3: וְהַלַּיְלָה אָמַר הֹרָה גָבֶר. Decontextually, it can

- The angel in charge of the winds is named "Duma" (דומה)[5]
- The angel in charge of rage (חימה) is named "Mehuman" (מהומן)[6]
- The angel in charge of 12,000 angels of destruction is named "Kemuel" (קמואל)[7]
- The angel in charge of anger (אף) is named "Distant" (רחוק)[8]
- The angel in charge of Israel is Michael.[9]

Other, unnamed, angels are cited according to their responsibilities, including:

- An angel in charge of souls[10]
- An angel in charge of desire[11]
- An angel in charge of prayers[12]
- An angel in charge of the form (alt: formation) of a fetus[13]
- An angel in Gehinnom who transfers circumcised Jews to the Garden of Eden[14]
- An angel who admits the dead to the Garden of Eden[15]
- An angel in charge of charity.[16]

---

be read, "Night said, a male was conceived." In context, Job is ruing the day he was born and the night at which someone announced his conception.

5. BT *Sanhedrin* (94a). See Isaiah 21:11.
6. *Midrash Abba Gurion* (ed. Buber), 1. See Esther 1: 10.
7. *Pesikta Rabbati* (ed. Ish-Shalom), 20. Elsewhere (Eisenstein, *Otzar Midrashim*), he is also called "the gatekeeper" (השוער).
8. *Midrash Tehillim* (ed. Buber), Psalm 5. See Isaiah 13:5.
9. *Pesikta Zutreta* (*Midrash Lekach Tov*), Exodus 23.
10. *Avot de-Rabbi Natan* A, 4.
11. *Bereishit Rabbah, VaYera* 53.
12. *Shemot Rabbah, Beshallach* 21.
13. *Midrash Tanchuma, Toledot* 6. The task is either יצירת הולד or צורת הולד.
14. *Midrash Tanchuma, Tzav* 14.
15. *Midrash Tanchuma, Tazria* 5.
16. *Midrash Tehillim* (ed. Buber), Psalm 88.

Perhaps the best known of all talmudic angels is the "angel of death" (מלאך המות). While absent in the Mishnah and Tosefta, it appears about ten times in *Bereishit Rabbah*, twice in other tannaitic midrashim,[17] well over 100 times throughout the rest of the Midrash Rabbah, about 15 times in the Babylonian Talmud and yet only once in the entire Jerusalem Talmud (*Shabbat* 2:5). This may indicate a particularly Babylonian-Persian provenance for Jewish concern about, and preoccupation with, angels – or with death.

In a relatively late (probably medieval) midrashic compilation called "The Book of Metatron," we find a veritable panoply of angels whose names are derivatives of their assignments:

> These are the names of the officers (שרים) who conduct the world:

- Gabriel, גבריאל, the angel of fire
- Bardiel, ברדיאל, the angel of hail
- Ruchiel, רוחיאל, the angel in charge of the wind
- Barkiel, ברקיאל, the angel in charge of lightning
- Zaʻmiel, זעמיאל, in charge of wrath
- Zikiel, זקיאל, in charge of sparks
- Zevaʻel, זועיאל, in charge of monstrosities
- Zaʻfiel, זעפיאל, in charge of gruffness
- Raʻmiel, רעמיאל, in charge of thunder
- Raʻshiel, רעשיאל, in charge of earthquakes
- Shilgiel, שלגיאל, in charge of snow
- Matriel, מטריאל, in charge of rains
- Shamshiel, שמשיאל, in charge of the day
- Layliel, ליליאל, in charge of the night
- Galgeliel, גלגליאל, in charge of the orbit of the sun

---

17. *Mekhilta, BaChodesh* 9; *Sifrei Nitzavim* 305.

- Ofniel, אופניאל, in charge of the orbit of the moon
- Kokhviel, כוכביאל, in charge of the stars
- Rahatiel, רהטיאל, is in charge of the constellations.[18]

Other late Midrashim also take note of:

- An [anonymous] angel in charge of judgment[19]
- An angel in charge of remembering, named Azkriel (אזכריאל).[20]

Geonim and Rishonim

Additional angels are cited by the authorities of the High Middle Ages.

In a geonic responsum, we learn of an anonymous angel who is in charge of taking note of merits (לכתוב זכיות) and another – of demerits (לכתוב חובות).[21] Each is described as "recording in pen" (כותב בקולמוסו).

Rashi cited some of the talmudic angels and added some of his own, including "Ridiya" (רידייא), who is in charge of providing rain to nourish the earth,[22] "B'ri" (ברי), the angel in charge of clouds,[23] and an anonymous angel responsible for rationing food (לזמן מזונות).[24] The Tosafot have but a single pertinent comment; namely, that "there is no angel in charge of parturition" (על הלידה אין שום מלאך ממונה).[25]

---

18. J.D. Eisenstein: *Otzar Midrashim* (NY, 1956). Metatron, aka "Minister of the Interior" (שר הפנים), is identified here with Enoch, of whom the Torah said: "Enoch walked with God and he was no more for God took him" (Genesis 5:24).
19. Eisenstein: *Otzar Midrashim*; "Marganita d'vei Rav."
20. Eisenstein: *Otzar Midrashim*; "Moshe." Also *Yalkut Shimoni, VaYelekh.*
21. *Teshuvot ha-Geonim Mussafia* (Lyk), 13.
22. *Yoma* (21a), *Ta'anit* (25b).
23. Job 37:11. This identification was already made by the 6–7th century paytan Eliezer Kalir who – in what has come to be known colloquially as *tefillat geshem* – declared b'ri to be "the name of the officer [in charge of] the rain (*sar matar*)."
24. *Pesachim* (111b).
25. *Nidah* 16b.

Nahmanides mentioned the angel "Ridiya," who was mentioned previously by Rashi, and added an anonymous angel in charge of "removing sin and atoning for transgression" (הסרת העון וכפרת החטא).[26] Menahem Recanati (Italy, 1250–1310) mentioned an anonymous angel in charge of trees.[27] Several additional angels were mentioned by Rabbi Isaac Aboab (Spain, 14th century), including an angel of judgment, an angel who darkens a person's face at death, and one who takes the lives of young men. In general, he stated: "There is an angel in charge of every single thing" (שעל כל דבר ודבר מלאך ממונה).[28]

R. Abraham Klausner (Vienna, 1340–1409) acknowledged an angel "in charge of writing" (הכתיבה) whose name he adduced as ספריאל (Safriel).[29] The Maharil (R. Jacob Moelin; Germany, 1365–1427) mentioned an angel named "Chatakh" (חת״ך) in charge of oaths, whose name is an acronym for his three responsibilities: חליפתי, תמורתי, כפרתי, terms that signify items that are exchanged for vows.[30]

R. Eliezer of Worms

Special significance attaches to the *Rokei'ach* (R. Eliezer of Worms; Germany, 1176–1238) who offered a most elaborate and detailed list of angels. In one of his works, entitled *Sodei Raziya* ("Enigmas Wrapped in Riddles"), he observed that "all the angels are named for their responsibilities" (כי כל המלאכים נקראים על שם מה שממונים עליו),[31]

---

26. *Ha-Emunah ve-ha-Bitahon*, chapters 3 and 20.
27. Commentary, Deuteronomy 16:21.
28. *Menorat ha-Ma'or*, chapters 3 (repentance), 20 (manners) and 1 (charity).
29. *Sefer ha-Minhagim* #15. The identification of that writing with the inscription of individual and collective destiny during the Days of Awe is discussed below.
30. *Minhagim*, laws of the eve of Yom Kippur. R. Jacob Weil (Germany, 15th century): *Responsa* #192, however, calls him "the angel in charge of life," which is also how he is known in the *Mishnah Berurah* (#605). The three specific Hebrew terms may be familiar from the *kapparot* ceremony in which many engage on the eve of Yom Kippur
31. Ed. Jerusalem, 2004; Part I, #30.

citing as evidence Rahatiel, רהטי״אל,³² in charge of comets, and Raziel, רזי״אל,³³ in charge of secrets. He also assigned an angel to each of the months:

- Shefa'iel, שפעי״אל, in charge of Nisan
- Ragi'ael, רגיע״אל, in charge of Iyyar
- Arina'or, ארינאו״ר [alt: Idana'or, אידנאו״ר], in charge of Sivan
- Ta'atzbun, תעצבו״ן [alt: Ta'anakhun, תענכו״ן], in charge of Tammuz
- Terodgar, תרודגא״ר [alt: Adurgar, אדורג״ר], in charge of Av
- Mor'el, מורא״ל, in charge of Elul
- Fahadarun, פהדרו״ן [alt: Pachadarun, פחדרו״ן], in charge of Tishrei
- Yalarang, ילרנ״ג [alt: Yalarbag, ילרב״ג], in charge of Heshvan
- Arbagdur, ארבגדו״ר [alt: Arangur, ארנגור], in charge of Kislev³⁴
- Abrekhiel, אברכי״אל, in charge of Adar, is so named on account of blessing (*berakhah*) and is also in charge of several additional angels of beneficence: Rumiel, רומי״אל; Hadriel, הדרי״אל; Chadshiel, חדשי״אל [alt: Charshiel, חרשי״אל]; Chasdiel, חסדי״אל; Safriel, ספרי״אל; Shlomiel, שלמי״אל; and Malkiel, מלכי״אל.

R. Eliezer also acknowledged the existence of the following angels:

- Nuriel, נורי״אל, the angel of fire
- Shamshiel, שמשי״אל, angel of the sun

---

32. From the Aramaic רה״ט, to run, implying fast-moving stars. The frequent (but not constant) use of the symbol " to separate the *aleph* from the *lamed* at the end of an angel's name is likely due to piety since E-L represents an epithet of God.
33. From the Aramaic רזא. An angel Raziel is well-known in kabbalistic literature.
34. Tevet and Shevat are skipped or missing.

- Yerachmiel, ירחמיא"ל, angel of the moon
- Kokhaviel, כוכביא"ל, angel of the stars
- Shofariel, שופריא"ל, the angel in charge of the "books of the living" (ספרי החיים)[35]
- Zekhutiel, זכותיא"ל, in charge of the merits of the people of Israel
- Yehudiel, יהודיא"ל in charge of all the angels[36]
- Amuel, the angel in charge of the curtain of the firmament (וילון הרקיע).[37]

He also refered to anonymous angels in charge of fire and water, and angels who serve the righteous in the Garden of Eden in the World to Come.[38]

Angels in Acharonim

R. Moshe Alshikh (Safed; early 17th century) named "Reshef" (רשף), the angel in charge of privation (יסורין).[39] R. Shlomo Ephraim Lunschitz (Prague; 1550–1619) mentioned an anonymous angel in charge of memory (זכרון).[40] Pinchas ha-Levi Horowitz (Poland and Germany; 1730–1805) stipulated that every mitzvah has an angel in charge of it (שעל כל מצוה יש מלאך ממונה על המצוה),[41] and also refered to an anonymous angel in charge of dreams.[42] Malbim (Meir Leib Weiser, Russia; 1809–1879) mentioned עיר, the angel in charge of implementation (להוציא הדבר אל הפועל) and קדיש, his superior, who influences him

---

35. I prefer to read "Shafriel" for reasons delineated below.
36. Ed. Jerusalem, 2004; Part I, #30.
37. Part I, #8.
38. Part II, entitled: "The Laws of Angels" (הלכות מלאכים).
39. Commentary on Habakkuk 3:5.
40. *Keli Yakar*, Deuteronomy 4:9.
41. *Panim Yafot*, Deuteronomy 25:9.
42. *Ibid.*, Genesis 37:17.

(המשפיע עליו).[43] Finally, Yechiel Michael ha-Levi Epstein (Lithuania, 1829–1908) cited Maharsha (R. Samuel Eidels; Poland, 1555–1631) to the effect that "there is no blade of grass without an angel above overseeing its growth" (אין לך כל עשב שלא יהיה לו מלאך מלמעלה הממונה על גדולו).[44]

Angels and Computing

Having catalogued Jewish angels and angelic tasks over the millennia, we may resume our speculation on whether the proliferation on earth of computers and the current preoccupation with computing, have their analogue in heaven.

We return, here, to the question that launched our inquiry: If God has indeed entered the cyber-age, which of His many ministering angels oversees the heavenly computer that records our deeds and prescribes our recompense? Obscured, perhaps, in the morass of angelological detail reported above, are the glimmerings of the answer we seek. Four of the sources we have cited pertain particularly to our question:

1. In a geonic responsum, we learn of one anonymous angel in charge of taking note of people's merits (לכתוב זכיות) and another – of their demerits (לכתוב חובות). Of more specific interest for our inquiry, each is described as "recording in pen" (כותב בקולמוסו).

2. A late Midrash took note of an anonymous angel in charge of judgment and an angel, named Azkriel (אזכריאל), who oversees remembering.

3. Eliezer Rokei'ach acknowledged Shafriel (שפריאל),[45] the angel in charge of the "books of the living" (ספרי החיים), whose name signifies anticipated or hoped-for glad tidings (אמרי שפר).

---

43. Commentary on Daniel 4:10.
44. *Torah Temimah*; Genesis 1, note 35. With the substitution of "constellation" (מזל) for "angel," it appears as early as *Bereishit Rabbah* and is cited, as such, by several medievals.
45. I prefer my reading to "Shofariel," since R. Eliezer noted that the phrase

4. Abraham Klausner (Vienna; 1340–1409) noted an angel whose name he adduced as ספריאל (Safriel). According to Klausner, he is "in charge of writing" (הכתיבה), by which he intended, specifically, the inscription of individual and collective destiny that is traditionally associated with the Days of Awe.

Each of these sources can serve as a precedent depending on our prior suppositions about technology.

A. If we view computing primarily as an efficient means of notetaking, then we should be prepared to be guided by the geonic precedent. The difference between manual record keeping (כותב בקולמוסו) and word processing is, philosophically, "accidental" rather than "essential." We would then argue to preserve the anonymity of the angels in charge, in keeping with the mundanity of their functions.

Such a minimalist view of computing is epitomized in the following critique:

> The Net's cacophony of stimuli short-circuits both conscious and unconscious thought, preventing our minds from thinking either deeply or creatively. Our brains turn into simple signal-processing units, quickly shepherding information into consciousness and then back out again.[46]

B. If we view computing as information storage and retrieval, a somewhat higher order function than mere word processing, then our pertinent precedent would be the midrashic reference to the angel in charge of remembering and the angel Azkriel would be in charge of computing, too.

A contemporary evaluation of this view of computing is forthcoming, as well:

אמרי שפר designates glad tidings. Nevertheless, the reference to "books of the living," a fixture of Rosh Hashanah lore, establishes a meaningful connection with the ram's horn.

46. Nicholas Carr: "The Juggler's Brain," *Phi Delta Kappan* 92:4 (Dec. 2010/Jan. 2011), 10.

> The depth of our intelligence hinges on our ability to transfer information from working memory to long-term memory and weave it into conceptual schemas.... [As] we reach the limits of our working memory, it becomes harder to distinguish relevant information from irrelevant information, signal from noise. We become mindless consumers of data.[47]

C. However, if we consider the dimension of "artificial intelligence" and regard computing not as a high-tech performance of essentially mechanical functions but as the execution of judgment and decision-making, then we will be led in another direction.

Indeed, given the geographical, chronological, and cultural proximity between Rokei'ach and Klausner, we would submit that Shafriel and Safriel are one and the same (a conclusion from which no authentic Litvak would demur). Furthermore, the more correct of the two versions is the latter, ספריאל, since it is supported by the gematria of the word עושה[48] (in the liturgical phrase that concludes the Amidah, עושה שלום במרומיו), without which there is no connection between the name of the supervisory angel and the function (inscribing destiny) he oversees.

Our conclusion, thus far, is that if the celestial record room has been computerized, and if the process followed therein is more than storage and retrieval of data but also includes evaluation and decision-making, then the likeliest angel to be presumed "in charge" of the operation would be ספריאל, literally "the bookish one" (and, with all due deference to angelic honor, might we suggest the "nerdy" one?). Still outstanding, however, is the fundamental question we raised at the outset regarding the ostensible contradiction between computing, as a venture that is synonymous with multi-tasking, and the discrete nature of angelic tasking.

---

47. Ibid., 11.
48. Both equal 381, while the numerical value of שפריאל would be 621.

Multi-Tasking: Is It Good or Bad for the Jews?

As we indicated in our prologue, multi-tasking, "the apparent simultaneous performance of two or more tasks," is regarded as a quintessential, even indispensible feature of computing. Given the rabbinic caveat that a single angel may not perform more than one function, does this not altogether preclude angels from computing?

Methodologically, there are two ways to approach this question. We may either challenge the validity of the rabbinic proposition, or we may contest the value of multitasking for computer function. We shall do both.

The Rabbis and Abraham's Guests

The first appearance of angels in the Bible occurs at Abraham's tent. He personally received three visitors who are initially called "men" (אנשים; Genesis 18:2), but then, upon the arrival of two of them in Sodom, they are designated "angels" (מלאכים; 19:1) and subsequently revert back to being called "men" (19:10), which they remain through the end of the episode.

Rabbinic tradition epitomized here in Rashi's commentary, identified the three visitors as angels. It further accounted for the discrepancy in their numbers (initially three, later two) by assigning each an exclusive task.

> "Behold there were three men:" One to break the news to Sarah, one to overturn Sodom, and one to heal Abraham, because one angel cannot perform two missions.[49]

The problem is as follows: Since only one angel was assigned the task of destroying Sodom, yet two angels are reported to have arrived there, what was the function of that second angel? Rashi says it was to rescue Lot. That is good enough, as it goes, but it only prompts a

---

49. והנה שלשה אנשים - אחד לבשר את שרה, ואחד להפוך את סדום, ואחד לרפאות את אברהם, שאין מלאך אחד עושה שתי שליחיות.

follow-up question: If one angel can perform only one assignment, then how could either of the original angels also rescue Lot? Rashi, however, stipulated:

> [The angel] Raphael, who healed Abraham, went thence to rescue Lot.[50]

In other words, Rashi implied that healing and rescuing are not two entirely disparate functions, but are similar enough that even a single angel can perform them both.

Applying this proposition to our inquiry, we may suggest that even an individual angel can perform multiple complementary functions, with, perhaps, the proviso that they must be performed serially. Such tasks as recording good and bad deeds, recalling them, and calculating their commensurate reward or punishment, can be seen as complementary functions and assigned to but a single angel.

Multi-Tasking: Much Ado About Little in Return

On the other hand, recent study indicates that the importance assigned to multitasking is disproportionate to its actual value. As Don Tapscott has written: "Most researchers take a dim view of multitasking. Psychological research has shown that our ability to do two things at once is limited."[51]

This negative appraisal is not only quantitative, it is also qualitative. Jordan Grafman, head of the cognitive neuroscience unit at the National Institute of Neurological Disorders and Stroke, wrote:

> Does optimizing [the brain] for multitasking result in better functioning – that is, creativity, inventiveness, productiveness? The answer is, in more cases than not, no... The more you multitask, the less deliberative you become; the less able to

---

50. ורפאל שרפא את אברהם הלך משם להציל את לוט.
51. Don Tapscott: *Grown Up Digital* (NY: McGraw-Hill, 2009), 107.

think and reason out a problem and the more you're willing to rely on stereotypical solutions.[52]

Multitasking is responsible for distraction from the principal task (as anyone who has answered a cell phone while driving can attest). Researchers from Stanford University found that:

> Heavy media multitaskers are more susceptible to interference from irrelevant environmental stimuli and from irrelevant representations in memory.... [The] human cognition is ill-suited both for attending to multiple input streams and for simultaneously performing multiple tasks.[53]

In contrast, these researchers found that "lower media multitaskers... have a greater tendency for top-down attentional control, and thus they may find it easier to attentionally focus on a single task in the face of distractions."[54]

Considering this growing body of research, multitasking, far from being a desirable trait to be nurtured, turns out to be a deficit to be avoided. If angels are constitutionally incapable of performing more than one assigned task at one time and can perform only complementary tasks serially, more power to them!

This, too, is anticipated in our classic sources. In his gloss on Maimonides, Raabad stated:

> Categorically, one person is incapable of directing his attention at two things at once, or [directing it] to two people at once who are engaged in separate activities (*Hilkhot Parah Adumah* 7:3).[55]

---

52. *Op. cit.*, 108–109.
53. Eyal Ophir, Clifford Nass, and Anthony D. Wagner: "Cognitive control in media multitaskers," *Proceedings of the National Academy of Sciences*, August 24, 2009, p. 1. Retrieved from: http://www.pnas.org/content/early/2009/08/21/0903620106.full.pdf, on 1/23/2011.
54. *Op. cit.*, p. 5.
55. 'וכללו של דבר אין אדם יכול לכוין דעתו לב' דברים כאחד או לשני בני אדם כא
נפרדים במעשיהם.

Conclusion

It seems, then, that whether God has replaced the angelic scriveners with computerized record keeping depends on how He perceives the principal function of computing.

If, indeed, He has done so, then it is likely that this cyber-activity is supervised by the Angel Safriel, who is invested with the responsibility – and ability – to distinguish between meritorious and detrimental deeds, to record them, and, finally, to award appropriate recompense – beneficent or malevolent – to their practitioners.

In consideration of this likelihood, instead of invoking the outdated paradigm of inscription and seal ("On Rosh Hashanah it is written, and on the fast of Yom Kippur it is sealed"), perhaps we should revise our High Holy Days' liturgy to recognize the latest advances in cyber technology. Appreciating the role of angels in celestial computer operations and assuming that heaven is as up to date as earth, a more suitable version might be:

"On Rosh Hashanah, our data is entered, and on Yom Kippur it is saved to the cloud."

Teshuvah, Tefillah, Tzedakah
Does What We Say Mean What We Think?

Preface
As the solemn *piyyut* of U-Netaneh Tokef reaches a crescendo, we recite: *u-teshuvah, u-tefillah, u-tzedakah ma'avirim et ro'a ha-gezeirah.*

With all due deference to most English translations, *teshuvah* is not "repentance," *tefillah* is not "prayer," *tzedakah* is not "charity," *le-ha'avir* is not "to abolish," and *ro'a ha-gezeirah* is not "the evil decree."

Etymology
"Repentance" derives from the same Latin root (*poena*[1]) that produces the words "penalty" and "penitentiary," and, as such, it complements the derivation of "sin" from the Anglo-Saxon for "evil," or "wickedness." The perpetration of evil incurs a penalty. However, no such pejorative connotation exists either in the Hebrew *cheit'*, "to miss (a goal),"[2] or *teshuvah*, literally, "return," which is better served, in this case, by "do-over." *Teshuvah*, then, signifies that if we miss the target, we are entiled to a second chance.

While "prayer," meaning "petition" (in Hebrew it would be *bak-*

---
1. As in "subpoena," which literally means "under penalty."
2. Cf. Judges 20:16: "Each [archer] could come within a hairsbreadth without missing [the mark]."

kashah), is a constituent part of *tefillah*, it is hardly synonymous with the whole enterprise, whose derivation from the verb *p-l-l*, "to judge," suggests self-judgment or introspection.

Finally, "charity," from the Latin *caritas* (love), implies an interpersonal relationship based entirely upon subjective emotions. The Hebrew *tzedakah*, to the contrary, preserves the root significance of "just," or "righteous," implying a more objective basis for that relationship.[3]

In spite of the objections I have raised here to the traditional translations, I will continue to use such words as "prayer," "repentance," and "sin" in their colloquial, normative, sense. By challenging their precision, I do not intend to emend the prayer book but to sharpen our awareness to both linguistic and theological nuances.

Can the "Evil Decree" Ever Be "Abolished"?

It is the translation of the continuation of the *piyyut*, however, which does the Hebrew the greatest injustice. To begin, "the evil decree," in Hebrew, would be *hagezeirah hara'ah*, and "to abolish" would be *levatteil*. Grammatically, *ro'a hagezeirah* is a construct, or possessive (*semikhut*), of two nouns and means the worst of the decree. *Ma'avirim*, from the verbal root *'avar*, "to pass or hover over," implies mitigation (or, temporary suspension) of judgment, rather than its complete annulment.[4]

Translated into programmatic terms, this means that the most that we can expect to happen to a decree that is enacted on account of our guilt is a suspension of its worst effects. We cannot anticipate the total abolition of consequences of deeds for which we ourselves are responsible. As the Sages maintained: "One who would sin and repent is not provided with the opportunity" (Mishnah, *Yoma* 8:9).

---

3. Chief Rabbi Jonathan Sacks, in *Covenant and Conversation* for *Parashat Re'eih*, calls *tzedakah* "The Untranslatable Virtue."
4. Cf. Micah 7:18: *'over 'al pesha'*; "to bear with (=tolerate) iniquity."

Were it otherwise, there would be no demonstrable advantage to strict observance of the law over its transgression.

Lest this appear to be "pop" theology, let me hasten to cite as evidence the commentary of Rashi on the conclusion of the text that is the focus of the remainder of this study: the proclamation of God's attributes in Exodus 34:6–7. In interpreting the oddly ambivalent phrase: "clearing [the slate], he clears [it] not" (*ve-nakkeih lo yenakkeih*), Rashi noted: "According to the plain sense it signifies that He never entirely exonerates the transgressor, but He requites him incrementally." Rashi, too, was opposed to the suggestion that a guilty party could reasonably expect to get off scot-free.

Is There a "Formula" for Pardon?

The second horn of our conceptual dilemma is contained in the following statement by Rabbi Yohanan concerning the thirteen attributes of God:

> "The Lord passed before him [Moses] and declared..." Rabbi Yohanan said: Were it not an explicit verse, we would not dare to declare it! God enveloped Himself like the emissary of the congregation [*shali'ach tzibbur*] and demonstrated to Moses an order of prayer, saying: Whenever the Jewish people sin... let them perform this order before me, and I shall pardon them (*Rosh Hashanah* 17b).

Here, we encounter a theme contrary to the one that we just developed, namely that there exists an "order of prayer" whose mere recitation is guaranteed to attain God's pardon.

Which of the two, then, is correct? Can we anticipate, as Rabbi Yohanan had it, the complete exoneration of sin, or, as we maintained earlier with the tacit support of Rashi, does God never totally exculpate the transgressor?

A Digression: God Enveloped as a Shali'ach Tzibbur

Whence did Rabbi Yohanan evoke the imagery of a *shali'ach tzibbur*? I believe it is partly literary and partly metaphorical. Literarily, the phrase: "He passed…before him" (*va-ya'avor al panav*) (Exodus 34:6) strongly resembles the mishnaic idiom: "to pass before the Ark" (*la'avor bifnei ha-teivah*), which designates the function of a *shali'ach tzibbur*.

The metaphorical part concerns the missing ingredient of a *teivah*, the Ark of the Law. I believe that it is represented in Rabbi Yohanan's proof text by Moses himself, who was secluded in the cleft of the rock grasping the two tablets of the covenant – the contents of the original *teivah*. This comparison is not without precedent; it is reminiscent of the profound declaration of the Amora Rava:

> How foolish are those people who rise before a Torah scroll but not before a great sage (*Makkot* 22b).

Consequences of the Golden Calf

Moses descended from Mt. Sinai, witnessed the frivolity that accompanied the sin of the golden calf, and smashed the first tablets to pieces. God threatened the Israelite nation with annihilation and Moses successfully interceded on its behalf. After the Levites exacted a partial retribution from the wrongdoers, God indicated His continuing displeasure by stipulating that only an angel would accompany them henceforth. He added, ominously, that "On the day of My accounting (*pakdi*), I will debit them (*pakadti*) for this sin (32:34).

Note, in passing, that the plain sense of this verse is consistent with the theology that we advocated of divine punishment being suspended rather than annulled. As Rashi commented here:

> At this moment, I have complied with your wish not to annihilate them completely. In the future, however, whenever I settle with them on account of their [recent] sins, I will debit them, slightly, on account of this sin, too.

Indeed, Rashi's continuing remark is a working theology of Jewish persecution:

> Every catastrophe that befalls the Jewish people is partial retribution for the sin of the golden calf.

Bear in mind that Rashi was contemporary not only to isolated exiles and persecutions, but also to the more severe and widespread massacres of the First Crusade.[5]

Seeking Atonement

Moses appealed to God to specify, more precisely, the nature of His continued association with the Jewish people. In so doing, Moses presumed upon his continued favor in God's eyes, coupled with God's singular relationship with him that he described as "knowing [him] by name" (Exodus 33:12). God acknowledged both the continuing favor and the special acquaintance (33:17) and promised to "proclaim the name of the Lord" before him (33:19).

Having instructed Moses to "station yourself there for me" (*ve-nitzavta li sham*) upon the mountain (34:2), God reciprocally "stationed Himself there with him" (*va-yityatzev 'immo sham*) and "proclaimed His name"[6] (34:5), just as He had promised earlier (33:19). He then proceeded to "pass before him [Moses]" as in Rabbi Yohanan's aforementioned "formula," and, with Moses secreted in the cleft of the rock, He made the proclamation of His thirteen attributes (34:6–7).

In reflecting on the reciprocal nature of our relationship with God during the month of Ellul, in particular, the Sages drew upon the verse: "I am my beloved's and my beloved is mine" (Song of Songs 6:3), whose

---

5. Rashi lived from 1040–1105 and the First Crusade lasted from 1095–1099. Cf. Yitzhak Baer: "Rashi and the Historical Reality of his Era" (Heb.), *Tarbitz* 20 (1949).
6. The cantillation marks (*ta'amei ha-mikra'*) indicate that verse should be read: *va-yikra' be-shem / Hashem*; making God the subject of the proclamation of His own name just as He is the subject of the prior descending and stationing.

initial Hebrew letters spell out the name of the month. This reciprocity is epitomized by the choreography of the *shali'ach tzibbur*, the opened *aron hakodesh*, and the recitation of the *shelosh esreih middot* that duplicates the circumstances of that original revelation.[7]

---

7. Cf. Moshe Sokolow: "The Thirteen Attributes; A Lesson in Atonement," in Daniel Z. Feldman, Stuart W. Halpern (eds.): *From Within the Tent; The Festival Prayers* (NY: YU Press, 2017), 29–40.

Shalom Aleikhem Mal'akhei Rachamim
When Yom Kippur Falls on Shabbat

Preface
The refrain Shalom Aleikhem, sung on Friday nights at the start of the Shabbat meal well-nigh universally, is surprisingly controversial. Some authorities have expressed reservations concerning the propriety of seeking a blessing from angels (*barkhuni le-shalom*) who, ostensibly, possess no will or capacity of their own, but are constrained to do only that which God instructs them.[1]

Similar misgivings have been voiced regarding several of the *selichot* and *piyyutim* recited during the *yamim ha-nora'im*, accounting for the title of this chapter.

Origins
According to the Talmud:

> Two ministering angels accompany a person home from the synagogue on the eve of Shabbat, one good and the other evil. If he returns home and finds candles burning, a set table, and a bed prepared, the good angel says, "May it be this way next Shabbat," and the evil angel reluctantly says, "Amen." Otherwise,

---
1. See "Angels Dancing on a Silicon Chip," above.

the evil angel says, "May it be this way next Shabbat," and the good angel reluctantly says, "Amen" (*Shabbat* 119b).

It is to these ministering angels (*mal'akhei ha-shareit*) that Shalom Aleikhem is traditionally sung. The poem itself first appeared in a book called *Tikkunei Shabbat* (Prague, 1641), whose title hints at a kabbalistic orientation, and, indeed, it is attributed to the circle of mystics of Safed in the 16–17th centuries among whose more famous members were Joseph Karo, Shlomo HaLevi Alkabetz, and Moses Cordovero. Its actual author, however, remains unknown.

The Reservations

For some, the solution was syntactical. In the *Siddur 'Avodat Yisra'el* (Roedelhiem, 1901), for instance, the text appears as follows:

שָׁלוֹם עֲלֵיכֶם מַלְאֲכֵי הַשָּׁרֵת מַלְאֲכֵי עֶלְיוֹן מֶלֶךְ מַלְכֵי הַמְּלָכִים הַקָּדוֹשׁ בָּרוּךְ הוּא:

Welcome to you, ministering angels, messengers of the most exalted, the king of kings, the Holy One, blessed is He.

The reasoning behind this variation (i.e., מֶלֶךְ rather than מִמֶּלֶךְ) was supplied by R. Halfon Moshe Ha-Cohen (Tunisia; 1874–1950), when he was asked:

> Is it proper to recite in Shalom Aleikhem "[Welcome...] angels of the exalted, from the King of Kings [*mi-melekh*...]," or [should one say]: "[Welcome] angels of the exalted, the King of Kings [*melekh*...]"?

He replied:

> In the first stanza, both options are intelligible, but in the remaining stanzas it is inconceivable to say "from," rather only "the King." That being the case, even the first should be "the King," so that they are all uniform. Furthermore, the greeting is being extended from man to the angels, not from God to

the angels, so how could one say "[Welcome...] from the King"?

Therefore, it is correct and appropriate to say "the King," as though to say: "angels of the exalted, [namely] the King of Kings..." So had I been accustomed, erroneously, to say "from the King" throughout, until I recanted and now I say "the King" throughout. Even if it says "from" in the prayer books, one should pay them no mind since printers, by and large, are unreliable (*Sho'eil ve-Nish'al* 11, *Orach Chayyim* 2).

Yom Tov on Shabbat

When a festival fell on Shabbat, however, the tendency was to omit Shalom Aleikhem. For some, the matter was strictly one of practicality. R. Yosef Hayyim b. Eliyahu al-Hakam (Iraq; 1835–1909), for instance, wrote:

> It is our practice at home when Yom Tov falls on Shabbat to circle twice and smell myrtle, as on other Sabbaths, to recite Shalom Aleikhem, Eishet Chayyil, and Yehei Ra'ava, and to arrange twelve loaves [of bread], as on other Sabbaths... Only if the first night of Passover falls on Shabbat, we do not recite Shalom Aleikhem and Eishet Chayyil...perhaps because we are obliged to hasten on Passover to recite Kiddush immediately... So it is also our custom when Rosh Hashanah falls on Shabbat to omit Shalom Aleikhem and Eishet Chayyil (*Rav Pe'alim* 1:13).

For others, like R. Yekutiel Yehudah Halberstam (Galicia and Israel; 1904–1995), it was a matter of abiding principle:

> In *Pesachim* (102b), Rashbam explains that one possesses an extra soul on Yom Tov, too, and the Tosafot challenge him pointing out that were this the case, why is there no blessing on spices [during *havdalah*] following Yom Tov? From this they deduce that one does not possess an extra soul on Yom Tov....

According to Rashbam, it is necessary to say that even if one possesses an extra soul on Yom Tov and one is accompanied [home from the synagogue] by angels, they are – in any event – of lesser stature than the Shabbat angels. In that case, when Yom Tov falls on Shabbat, it is conceivable that one is accompanied by four angels – two of Shabbat and two of Yom Tov.

It is possible even according to the Tosafot – who say there is no extra soul on Yom Tov – that on Yom Tov one is accompanied by other guardian angels. Yet, because one does not greet Yom Tov angels…we do not recite [Shalom Aleikhem] at all when Yom Tov falls on Shabbat (*Divrei Yatziv, Orach Chayyim* 123).

Angels and Intercession: Shouldn't We Speak to God Directly?

The Talmud accepts the notion that intercessory powers "above" are available to assist those who entreat from "below." Conversely, those "below" who fail to pray properly will encounter opposition from "above."

> Reish Lakish said: "Whoever strives to pray from below has no opposition above." R. Yohanan said: "One should always implore for compassion that all may support his effort in prayer, so that he shall have no opposition above" (*Sanhedrin* 44b).

Rashi interpreted this to mean:

> Whoever strives to pray from below: The opposition cannot bedevil him from above. One should ever implore compassion that all may support his effort: That the ministering angels should assist him to seek compassion so that he will not be bedeviled from above.

R. Shmuel Strashun (Lithuania; 1784–1872), a talmudic glossator, applied this to the liturgy of the Yamim Nora'im:

From this we can obtain support for the recitation of the *pizmon* [song or poem] of *mal'akhei rachamim*[2]...and such similar items over which many have been hesitant. However, it is likely that it is permissible [to address them] only [when praying] in private....

Shalom Aleikhem, Rav Moshe

Rabbi Moshe Feinstein (Lithuania and U.S.A.; 1895–1986) expressed his reservations about Shalom Aleikhem within the context of the propriety of addressing angels, particularly during the Yamim Nora'im. He wrote:

With respect to our finding in liturgical poems [*piyyutim*] and penitential prayers [*selichot*] that we ask angels to pray for us, such as Angels of Compassion [*mal'akhei rachamim*] or Attributes of Compassion [*middat ha-rachamim*], there appears to be a difference of opinion. The authors of the *piyyutim*, who were great sages, introduced this custom, but many of the later sages prohibit it.... The *Chatam Sofeir* himself would recite *selichot* along with the congregation, but when they got to *makhnisei rachamim* he would prolong his recitation of tachanun in order to avoid saying it....[3]

---

2. Literally: "Angels of compassion," alternatively: "Compassionate angels."
3. The reference is to R. Moshe Sofer (Pressburg; 1762–1839). In *Orach Chayyim* 166, he wrote:

> ...he questions the Gaon, the Maharal of Prague (1512–1609)...who declined to recite the *piyyut* of *makhnisei rachamim* because we have no dealings with angels but with God, who hears all prayers. The *Peri Megadim* (Germany; 1727–1793) [similarly] argued that all the biblical books are filled with [such things as] "she [Rebecca] went to seek out God" (Gen. 25:22).
>
> I shall explain that it is customary to place an intermediary between a king and a commoner whenever the commoner has no significance before the king, or if he cannot express himself appropriately. Since [the People of] Israel are closer to God than the ministering angels

We find that the *Siddur Iyyun Tefillah* emended *mal'akhei rachamim chalu na'* [compassionate angels, entreat; i.e., in the imperative] to read *yechalu na'* [they entreat].[4] I recall that my father would never say anything resembling a request of angels. Instead of *mal'akhei rachamim*, he would say *avot ha-'olam ahuvei 'Elyon, chalu na'* ["venerable ancestors, beloved of the Exalted One, please entreat"] and during *Selichot* and *Ne'ilah* he would say, "the attribute of compassion has encompassed us" [rather than: "encompass us"] and "our petition has been cast before our Creator" [rather than: "cast our petition before"] and "compassion has been sought on behalf of our nation" [rather than: "seek compassion"]" – even though it goes against the rhyme scheme – and I follow in his custom.

Lately I have seen in the *Siddur Otzar Tefillot* that R. Hayyim Volozhin would also make substitutions, such as "venerable ancestors entreat" instead of "angels of compassion," and it is possible that my father got his cue from R. Hayyim Volozhin. For the same reason, my father would not recite the stanza of "bless me in peace" when reciting Shalom Aleikhem on the eve of Shabbat. (*Iggerot Moshe; Orach Chayyim* 5:43)

... and Rav Ovadyah, Too

Lest we imagine these reservations to be the exclusive property of Eastern European rabbinic intricacies, let us hasten to note that they are expressed by Rav Ovadyah Yosef (Egypt, Israel; 1920–2013) as well:

> Regarding the prayer of Mal'akhei Rachamim, wherein we pray to angels, we see in *Ma'aseh Rav* that the Gaon of Vilna ques-

---

are, they do not require such an intermediary before God who accepts their prayers graciously – even if they stutter and mumble. That being the case, turning to an intermediary is a sign of little faith.

4. Thereby eliminating the problem of petitioning angels.

tioned this practice. Similarly, [he questioned saying] "bless us with peace" [*barekhuni le-shalom*] on the eve of Shabbat, because the angels have no power, neither can they exercise choice.... Even though the verse does speak of "intercessory angels" (Job 33:23), it still depends upon one's behavior. When one has merit, an angel is created from his good deeds and will surely serve as his intercessor. [Yet] he said that as long as he remembers, he never said *barekhuni le-shalom* on the eve of Shabbat, nor *mal'akhei rachamim* during *selichot*.

However, R. Yisrael Bruna (Germany; 1400–1480) explains in his responsa that this is only an expression of modesty and self-abasement by asking the king's courtiers to address the king on his behalf while he is embarrassed to approach the king personally. This does not constitute an intermediary at all. (*Yabia' 'Omer* vol. I, *Orach Chayyim* 35)

Epilogue

Whenever Yom Kippur would fall on Shabbat, my father, *a"h*, would make a point of singing Shalom Aleikhem upon our return home from *Kol Nidrei* services. He had acquired this custom from his father-in-law, the Chazan Judah Appel, who, I have surmised, had seen it practiced amongst the Vishnitzer Hasidim with whose *rebbe* he had shared a school bench as a boy. The custom piqued my curiosity and this discussion represents my attempt to satisfy it.

Thanksgiving: A Heimische Holiday After All
How the Pilgrims Came to Recite Birkat Ha-Gomeil

A History of the Holiday

In 1789, in response to a resolution offered by Congressman Elias Boudinot of New Jersey, President George Washington issued a proclamation recommending that Thursday, November 26th of that year

> be devoted by the people of these States to the service of that great and glorious Being who is the beneficent author of all the good that was, that is, or that will be; that we may then all unite in rendering unto Him our sincere and humble thanks for His kind care and protection of the people of this country previous to their becoming a nation.

In New York City, Congregation Shearith Israel convened a celebration on that day at which its minister, Gershom Mendes Seixas, embraced the occasion:

> As we are made equal partakers of every benefit that results from this good government; for which we cannot sufficiently adore the God of our fathers who hath manifested his care over us in this particular instance; neither can we [sufficiently]

demonstrate our sense of His benign goodness, for His favourable interposition in behalf of the inhabitants of this land.

While the celebrations at this venerable Orthodox synagogue continue unabated, to this day, other American Jewish responses to Thanksgiving have ranged from the skeptical to the outright antagonistic. In an essay entitled "Is Thanksgiving Kosher?"[1] Rabbi Michael Broyde examined three halakhic (legal) positions on the subject: Rabbi Yitzhak Hutner, who ruled Thanksgiving a Gentile holiday and forbade any recognition of it; Rabbi Joseph B. Soloveitchik, who regarded it as a secular holiday but nonetheless permitted the celebration (particularly, eating turkey); and Rabbi Moshe Feinstein, who permitted turkey but prohibited any other celebration because of reservations over the recognition of even secular holidays.

Pilgrims, the Mayflower, and Giving Thanks

Newly presented historical information, however, may swing the annual autumnal pendulum more in favor of participation in what now appears to have been a holiday with a patent Jewish theme and performance. Nick Bunker, in his book *Making Haste from Babylon: The Mayflower Pilgrims and their World* (Random House/Knopf, 2010), revealed an item of particular significance for both Jewish observers and critics of Thanksgiving.

Fleeing from persecution in England, the Pilgrim passengers on the *Mayflower* brought along their principal source of religious inspiration and comfort: The Bible. One particular edition of the Bible (published in 1618) that is known to have been in the possession of none other than William Bradford, destined to serve as a governor of Plymouth colony, was supplemented by the annotations of a Puritan scholar named Henry Ainsworth (1571–1622).

Shortly after their landfall in November 1620, Bradford led the

---

1. http://www.tfdixie.com/special/thanksg.htm

new arrivals in thanking God for the safe journey that brought them to America by reciting verses from Psalm 107. Curiously, Ainsworth's annotations to verse 32 of that chapter, "Let them exalt him also in the congregation of the people, and praise him in the assembly of the elders" (King James), contains the following remarks (see facsimile):

> And from this Psalme, and this verse of it, the Hebrues have this Canon; Foure must confess (unto God) The sick, when he is healed; the prisoner when he is released out of bonds; they that goe down to sea, when they are come up (to land); and wayfaring men, when they are come to the inhabited land. And they must make confession before ten men, and two of them wise men, Psal. 107. 32.
> And the manner of confessing and blessing is thus; He standeth among them and blesseth the Lord, the King eternal, that bounteously rewardeth good things unto sinners, etc. Maimony in Misn. Treat. Of Blessings, chap. 10, sect. 8.

Hakarat Ha-Tov

If any of this looks familiar, it is because Ainsworth essentially copied over an English version of Maimonides's *Mishneh Torah* (Maimony Mis.), *Hilkhot Berakhot* (Treat[ise] of Blessings) 10:8, which prescribes the four conditions under which *Birkhat ha-Gomeil*, the blessing after being spared from mortal danger, is to be publicly recited. Citing additional verses from Psalm 107, Bradford compared the Pilgrims' arrival in America to the Jews crossing the Sinai Desert, corresponding to "wayfaring men, when they are come to the inhabited land," one of the four conditions requiring confession.

Bunker consequently argued that the very first prayer that the Pilgrims recited immediately upon their arrival in the New World had its origins in a distinctly Jewish practice. He goes on to write that he considers this prayer service to be the original "Thanksgiving" and that it took place a full year before the three days of feasting that serve as the basis for the current American holiday.

Even without turkey and cranberry sauce, this vestige of Jewish influence on the religious mores of our country, from its inception, deserves our acknowledgment and contemplation – and, of course, thanksgiving.

> 32   V. 32. *the sitting*]. or the *Assise (session) of the Elders*, or *Senators*, the governours of the people; whome the Chaldee calleth, *Wise men*. And from this Psalme, and this verse of it, the Hebrues have this Canon; *Foure must confess (unto God,) The sick, when he is healed; the prisoner when he is released out of bonds; they that goe down to sea, when they are come up (to land;) and wayfaring men, when they are come to the inhabited land. And they must make confession before ten men, and two of them wise men*, Psal. 107.31. *And the manner of confessing and blessing is thus; He standeth among them and blesseth the Lord, the King eternall, that bounteously rewardeth good things unto synners &c.* Maimony in Misn. treat. of Blssings, chap. 10. sect. 8.

Psalms 107:32, with
Ainsworth's annotations

VeTein Tal UMatar LiVerakhah
What Is so Holy About the 4th (or 5th or 6th) of December? Some Insights Into the Interplay Between the Calendar and the Liturgy

Preface

In this chapter, we will inquire into the basic outline and formation of the Jewish calendar and then explore the details of *Vetein Tal u-Matar* ("provide dew and rain"), the liturgical insert into the *Amidah* praying for rain. In the process, we will intersect with a variety of disciplines, including prayer, holidays, algebra, geography, astronomy, Jewish history, and comparative religions.

The Jewish Calendar – General Observations

A. SOLAR VS. LUNAR

Both the solar and the lunar cycles figure prominently in the Jewish calendar. As Maimonides stipulated:

> The months of the year are lunar, as it states: "The monthly *olah* each month" (Numbers 28:14) and it states: "This month shall be, for you, the first of the months" (Exodus 12:2). Our Sages said: "God displayed to Moshe, prophetically, the image of the

moon and said: 'When you see it thus [i.e., the sliver of the new moon] – sanctify it!'" [However,] the years that we reckon are solar years, as it states: "Keep the month of ripe barley" (Deuteronomy 16:1) (*Hilkhot Kiddush ha-Chodesh* 1:1).

In other words, the mitzvah of sanctifying the new month (*kiddush ha-chodesh*) requires lunar months, *chodashim*,[1] while the requirement to observe Passover during the barley season (*chodesh ha-'aviv*) can be maintained only via solar years.[2]

B. INTERCALATION (*'IBBUR HA-SHANAH*)

Since the duration of a solar year is 365¼ days, while that of a lunar year is only 354 days, it became necessary to "intercalate," or merge the two calendars, through a halakhic process called *'ibbur ha-shanah*. As Maimonides continued:

> How much does a solar year exceed a lunar year? About 11 days. Therefore, when this excess amounts to 30 days, or thereabouts, we add a month, and make that year a leap year [*shanah me'ubberet*] of 13 months. It is impossible to make a year of 12 months and however many extra days, because it states: "[This month shall be, for you, the first of the months; it shall be the first of]

---

1. The Hebrew noun *chodesh*, meaning "month," derives from the verbal root *ch-d-sh*, which means "to be new." Lunar months naturally renew themselves through the waxing and waning of the moon; hence, the noun "month" – from moon, just as Hebrew uses *yerach* – from *yare'ach* – as a synonym for *chodesh*.
2. The word *'aviv* is commonly mistaken for "spring." In reality, the Bible knows of only two – sharply contrasting – seasons, reflecting the climate of the Land of Israel. Witness God's promise to Noah: "As long as the earth shall last: sowing and reaping, cold and heat, summer and winter (*kayitz va-choref*), day and night, shall not cease" (Genesis 8:22). The use of *'aviv* in Deuteronomy 16 as a means of fixing the time for Passover follows the lead of Exodus 9:31–32. After the plague of hail that preceded the exodus from Egypt, we were informed that: "Flax and barley were stricken," because they were – at that time – already fully developed, while "wheat and buckwheat were not stricken, because they were [still] immature" and could bend in the storm.

the annual months" (Exodus 12:2). Years are comprised of months and not of individual days (*Hilkhot Kiddush ha-Chodesh* 1:2).

As a result, the typical Jewish year (*shanah peshutah*) consists of either 353 days (called *chaseirah*, "deficient"), 354 days (called *kesidra'*, "ordinary"), or 355 days (called *sheleimah*, "full"), depending upon whether the months of Marcheshvan and Kisleiv are 29 days each, 30 days each, or one is 29 and the other 30. The arrangement is based upon a series of fixed adjustments, called "postponements" (*dechiyyot*), which govern the scheduling of certain key holidays. Rosh Hashanah, for instance, cannot begin on Sunday, Wednesday, or Friday, and Passover cannot begin on Monday, Wednesday, or Friday.

Each year is designated by an abbreviation (*simanei kevi'ut*) identifying its length, and indicating the first day of each of these holidays. Bet-Shin-Hei, for example, identifies the year as a *sheleimah* (*shin*), with Rosh Hashanah on Monday (*bet*) and Passover on Thursday (*hei*). Zayin-Kaf-Alef means shana *kesidra'* (*kaf*), with Rosh Hashanah on Shabbat (*zayin*) and Passover on Sunday (*alef*).

The "leap" month (Adar II) is always inserted right before Nisan since its purpose – as explained by Maimonides above – is to prevent the holiday of Passover from slowly retreating into the winter. Consider the following: At the rate of 11 days per year, in 10 years' time the lunar and solar calendars would drift apart by 110 days. If Passover began one year, let us say, on April 15, ten years later – without adjustment – it would fall on December 25.

Since the leap month adds 30 days to the year, the rabbis instituted it approximately every three years, according to the formula: $30 \times X$ (representing the added month) $= 11Y$ (the days lost per year). $X=7$, $Y=19$ ($210 \approx 209$); hence, seven out of every 19 years (years 3, 6, 8, 11, 14, 17, and 19) are leap years. Each 19-year cycle (*machzor*) is called a "lunar cycle," or "minor cycle," while every 28 years complete a solar, or major cycle. The solar blessing (*Birkhat ha-Chamah*), recited every 28 years, marks the return of the sun to the identical position it occupied at the instant of its creation.

Jewish and Muslim Lunar Calendars Compared

A contrast to the "intercalated" Jewish calendar is provided by the Muslim calendar, which is also lunar, but not adjusted. Since it repeats the same number of days (354) year after year, two interesting results occur:

a. Unlike Passover and Sukkot, which are seasonally fixed, Muslim holy days – like the month of Ramadan – fall during widely divergent seasons of the year. (In *Jews and Arabs*, S.D. Goitein tells of the confusion and consternation with which the earliest Muslim travelers to Scandinavia greeted the strikingly different prospects of keeping a daylight fast during either the six months of night or the six months of day.[3])

b. Muslims seemingly age faster than Jews. When a Jew celebrates his 33rd birthday according to the Jewish calendar, a Muslim born on the same day will be celebrating his 34th birthday according to the Muslim calendar. This phenomenon also explains why the date according to the Muslim era (which commenced with Muhammad's emigration from Mecca to Medinah in 621–622 CE) cannot be determined by simply subtracting 622 from the current year.

Tal U-Matar: The Prayer for Rain
A. MISHNAH AND GEMARA
The Mishnah stipulates:

> On 3 Marcheshvan[4] we pray for rain. Rabban Gamliel said: On the seventh of the month, that is 15 days after the festival [of

---

3. For the record, the instruction they received was to fast or feast during the same hours of the day during which people in Mecca would be either fasting or feasting.
4. A common misconception derives *marcheshvan* from the verse: "Behold

Sukkot], in order to allow even the tardiest Israelite to reach the Euphrates (*Ta'anit* 1:3).

According to Rabban Gamliel (whose opinion prevails), the prayer for rain in the Land of Israel is delayed only long enough to give the last pilgrims time to reach the furthest boundary of the Land of Israel – which was with Syria – before they would be caught by the anticipated downpours. (Were there no pilgrims, we would surmise, this prayer – like the pronouncement of *mashiv ha-ru'ach* – would commence immediately after Shemini Atzeret.)

Outside of Israel, however, the practice differed, as the Gemara explains:

> Hananiah said: In the Diaspora [we do not begin] until the sixtieth day of the season (*Ta'anit* 10a).

B. MAIMONIDES' CODIFICATION

These two laws were codified by Maimonides as follows:

> From the seventh of Marcheshvan we insert the prayer for rain into the blessing for the years whenever we mention rain [i.e., until Passover]. This is in the Land of Israel, but in Mesopotamia, Syria, Egypt and nearby or similar places, we pray for rain on the sixtieth day of the Tishrei season [i.e., after the autumnal equinox] (*Hilkhot Tefillah* 2:16).

C. SEASONS (*TEKUFOT*) AND HEMISPHERES

There are four seasons to the solar year, corresponding to the four quadrants of the ellipse that describes the path the Earth takes in its revolutions around the sun. The following chart describes them:

---

the nations are but a drop (*mar*) in the bucket (*deli*)" (Isaiah 40:15), ostensibly signfying Cheshvan as the month in which it begins to rain in Israel. Another "folk" etymology associates it with the Hebrew word for bitter (*mar*), reflecting the absence of any holidays during that month. In reality, *marcheshvan* is a corruption of the words *yerach shemini*, "the eighth month" (when the count starts with Nisan).

	Northern Hemisphere	Southern Hemisphere
A. 22 March – 21 June	Spring (day longer than night)	Fall (night longer than day)
B. 22 June – 22 September	Summer (day longer than night)	Winter (night longer than day)
C. 23 Sept. – 22 December	Fall (night longer than day)	Spring (day longer than night)
D. 23 Dec. – 21 March	Winter (night longer than day)	Summer (day longer than night)

Now we can see the dimensions of the problem very clearly: Since the autumn (Tishrei) season commences on September 23 (in the Northern Hemisphere, which is our primary concern), then the sixtieth day thereafter is November 21. Why, then, do we not commence saying *Tal u-Matar* until December 4, which is thirteen days later?

Tal U-Matar: How We Arrived at December 4
A. THE PROBLEM WITH SHEMUEL'S CALCULATIONS

The determination of the equinox (*tekufah*) for the purposes of *Tal u-Matar* was originally made according to the rules of Ptolemaic astronomy as set down by the Amora Shemuel (Babylonia, 3rd century CE) – the same authority who ruled that the *halakhah* in the Diaspora follows Hananiah – namely: "The *tekufot* are separated by 91 days, 7 ½ hours" (*Eruvin* 56a).

Multiply 91 days 7 ½ hours times four seasons and the result is a year calculated to be exactly 365 days and 6 hours long. The problem, however, is that a more exact astronomical calculation of the length of a year – following Copernican astronomy – is 365 days, 5 hours, 48 minutes and 46 seconds: a difference of 11 minutes and 14 seconds. How long does it take – at this rate – to gain one day?

1,440 (minutes in a day: 60 × 24) ÷ 11 min. 14 sec. (11.25 hrs.)
= 128 years.

1,000 years ÷ 128 = 7.8 millennia

As the preceeding equation demonstrates, as a result of this annual discrepancy, every 128 years the halakhic *tekufah* moved forward one day, and about 8 full days every millenium. By the end of the 16th century – about 1,500 years after Shmuel – it had moved about 12 days, from September 23 to October 4.

B. POPE GREGORY AND THE NEW CALENDAR

Interestingly enough, the Catholic Church was the first to address this discrepancy. The Nicene Council, in 325 CE, had correctly fixed March 21 (the vernal equinox) as the date that would determine the Easter holiday. Each 128 years, as we explained, March 21 moved forward, relative to the sun, by one full day. By 1582, the discrepancy had reached 10 days.

Pope Gregory XIII decided to drop the extra ten days from the calendar by decreeing that the day after Thursday, October 4, 1582, would be Friday, October 15, in a new calendar named "Gregorian" in his honor.[5] To ensure that the problem remained corrected, Gregory also eliminated three leap years every 400 years (remember that – according to Shemuel – the *tekufah* moves forward one day every 128 years, and 3 × 128 = 384), namely, in the century years not divisible by 400. This results in an average year of 364.2425 days, at which rate it would now take 3,300 years to accumulate an extra day.

C. A LITTLE "JEWISH" MATH

The result of these alterations is that – by the twentieth century – the day that would have been September 23 according to the Julian (Shemuel's) calendar was October 7 of the Gregorian calendar, and the sixtieth day following October 7 is December 5. Since we begin reciting *Tal u-Matar* during the Ma'ariv service, it turns out to be said

---

5. We mark Washington's Birthday on February 22, even though he was born on February 11, because Britain and its colonies first adopted the Gregorian calendar after he was born. (http://www.archives.gov/legislative/features/washington/)

beginning with the night of December 4. Every fourth year, however (in the Jewish year divisible by four), the *tekufah* will begin after nightfall (*tzeit ha-kokhavim*) on October 7, so the sixtieth day during those years will be December 6, and *Tal u-Matar* will commence on the evening of December 5.

While the *tekufah* always falls on October 7, each year it begins 6 hours later – remember that it is still calculated according to Shemuel (and Julian) who assumed an exact 364¼ day year – so in each four-year cycle the *tekufah* begins, sequentially, at 3 a.m., 9 a.m., 3 p.m. and 9 p.m. – the latter being later than *tzeit ha-kokhavim*. (If you are wondering how the *tekufah* can always remain on October 7 when the year following 9 p.m. it should fall at 3 a.m. of October 8, remember that the year in which the *tekufah* comes at 9 p.m. is the year preceding a civil leap year which uses up the extra day.)

Since the year 2000 in the Gregorian calendar was a leap year, too, the December 4–5 dates will continue throughout the 21st century. However, since 2100 will not be a leap year (it is not divisible by 400), the *tekufah* in 2101 will move forward one day (to October 8), and *Tal u-Matar* will move to December 5–6.

This pattern repeats itself, so every 400 years Tal u-Matar is said three days later.

Problems for Europe and the Southern Hemisphere

Thus far, we have explained how the nuances of the Julian and Gregorian calendars determine the dates on which the prayer of *Tal u-Matar* is inserted into *Birkhat ha-Shanim*. However, one major problem remains.

The Gemara in *Ta'anit* (see above) stipulates the sixtieth day of the Tishrei season as the date for beginning *Tal u-Matar* in the Diaspora (*golah*), which refers specifically to Babylonia, and even Maimonides (see above) broadened the *halakhah* only enough to include Syria, Egypt, and countries nearby or with similar (climatological?) conditions. What about Europe and North America – let alone the entire Southern Hemisphere – whose climates are significantly different?

WHAT IS SO HOLY ABOUT THE 4TH OF DECEMBER? · 69

Should the Jews of Brazil or Australia pray for rain from December through April when their winter months are June-September (see the *tekufah* charts above)? Does it make any sense for the Jews of the United States to pointedly stop praying for rain on the first day of Passover when that is not too late – in some places – even for snow and, in any event, it continues to rain throughout the year?

A. MISHNAH AND GEMARA

To answer these questions, we must go back to the Gemara and return, via medieval and modern responsa, to the present. The Gemara, first, makes provision for different climates, allowing the prayer for *Tal u-Matar* to be inserted in the blessing of *Shomea' Tefillah*, rather than *Birkhat ha-Shanim*:

> The inhabitants of Nineveh [in Babylonia] inquired of Rebbi [R. Yehudah the Nasi]: We, who need rain even during the summer, how shall we act: As individuals [who insert their prayer] during *Shomea' Tefillah* or as a community [entitled to add the insert] during *Birkhat ha-Shanim*? Rebbi replied: You are regarded as individuals and [should pray for rain] during *Shomea' Tefillah* (*Ta'anit* 14b).

The Gemara rules according to Rebbi, but it also records the conflicting opinions of Rabbi Yehuda and Rav Nahman who permit local communities, such as Nineveh, to recite *Tal u-Matar* in *Birkhat ha-Shanim* at whatever time suits them best.

While it is clear, then, that Diaspora communities can say *Tal u-Matar* in *Birkhat ha-Shanim* only during their rainy season, it is unclear whether the Gemara intended them to follow the custom of Eretz Yisrael and begin on 7 Marcheshvan, or to follow Babylonian custom and begin on the sixtieth day of the *tekufah*. Furthermore, since – even with Nineveh – it only relates to the summer season in Eretz Yisrael, it still fails to resolve the dilemma created by the unique situation of the Southern Hemisphere.

We shall deal, here, with two representative examples: Provence and Brazil.

B. PROVENCE AND THE CUSTOM OF R. ASHER

In the Middle Ages we find in practice that Europe (and North Africa) followed the Babylonian custom, except for Provence (and the possible exception of Kairouan, Tunisia), which followed the custom of Eretz Yisrael. While their actual practices are well attested to, their origins are not, and it remains uncertain whether they were originally based upon talmudic exegesis or meteorology.

In other words, when Hananiah described the practice of Babylonia, he referred to it as "ha- Golah." Is that just an idiomatic expression, or was it intended all along to denote all Diaspora communities? On the other hand, it just so happens that in Provence (and Tunisia) the rainy season begins in September or October.

The Provencal custom is reported approvingly by R. Asher in his commentary on *Ta'anit* (12b) as follows:

> I am surprised that we follow the Babylonian practice in this regard. While our Talmud is Babylonian, the matter (of praying for rain) depends upon the Land (of Israel). Why should we not follow their custom? Even if Babylonia has abundant water and does not need rain, other countries need rain in Marheshvan so why delay the prayer until the sixtieth day of the season? Why should we not follow the ruling of the Mishnah? In Provence I have seen that they pray for rain beginning with Marheshvan and I heartily approve.

R. Asher, in fact, not only argued for starting *Tal u-Matar* in Marcheshvan, but, in a responsum (4:10) he wrote in 1313, he argued that the prayer could be continued even beyond Passover and all the way to Shavu'ot, if local conditions warranted it. This opinion, however, was rejected even by his son, R. Yaakov, in the *Tur*, and the phraseology of the *Shulchan Arukh* dispels all the ambiguity that inheres in the talmudic term "Golah" by stating categorically: "Outside of the Land of Israel one begins the prayer... on the sixtieth day of the autumn season" (*Orach Chayyim* 117:1).

To contrast two more recent opinions, Abraham Geiger, the Reform leader, ruled that German Jews might say *Tal u-Matar* all year round, while the *Arukh ha-Shulchan* (perhaps in reaction?) stipulated: "Whoever doubts the law [decided in the *Shulchan Arukh*] deserves to be punished," and, referring to the rejection of the decision of R. Asher, he added:

> Since R. Asher himself acknowledged that his opinion was not accepted, it is as though a heavenly voice (*bat kol*) ruled to follow Babylonian custom.

C. THE SOUTHERN HEMISPHERE

Interestingly, the first question of religious law (*she'elah*) to be sent back to Europe from the "New World" concerned *Tal u-Matar*.

The first Jewish settlement in the New World was established, in 1637, in the Portuguese colony of Recife, near Brazil, and one of the first religious problems encountered was reckoning the proper time to say *Tal u-Matar*. On the one hand, the settlers were accustomed to following the Babylonian tradition, which had won out, time and again, over all attempts – such as that of R. Asher – to modify it in accordance with local conditions. On the other hand, however, was the overwhelming illogic of praying for rain during Brazil's summer, and foregoing the prayer precisely when rain was needed, just because the tradition was founded in another era and a different hemisphere.

Congregation Zur Yisrael raised this question in a letter to Rabbi Hayyim Shabbetai of Salonica, whose answer set the precedent by which most of the Jews of South America and Australia abide to this very day. Basing himself upon the opinions of Maimonides (one, in his commentary to Mishnah *Ta'anit*, and the other, in the *Mishneh Torah, Tefillah* 2:17), and taking the responsum of R. Asher into consideration, Rabbi Shabbetai ruled that since during the months of Nisan through

Tishrei prayers for rain may be recited only in *shomea' tefillah* (as individuals), and since one should not have to pray for rain at a time at which it would be harmful for him, the Jews of Brazil should:

a. never say *Tal u-Matar* in *Birkhat ha-Shanim*;
b. never even say *mashiv ha-ru'ach u-morid ha-geshem*[6];
c. say *Tal u-Matar* in *Shomea' Tefillah* during their rainy season, as needed.

While the addition of *Ve-Tein Tal u-Matar li-V'rakhah* constitutes the entire prayer for rain in the Ashkenazic liturgy, the Sephardic prayer for rain (in the Northern Hemisphere) actually changes the entire text of *Birkhat ha-Shanim*. It may be of interest to note, in closing, that since South American Sephardic Jews do not say *Tal u-Matar* in *Birkhat ha-Shanim* at all, many of them have never seen that rainy season version.

---

6. All manuscripts and printed *siddurim* prior to 1787 have *geshem*. The change to *gashem* was introduced by Isaac Satanov, infamous for his publication of books that he falsely attributed to famous authors who had not written them, in a *siddur* he printed in that year in Berlin.

Neir Chanukkah: VeHeikhan Tzivvanu?
Is the Mitzvah of Hanukkah Lights *DeOraita* or *DeRabanan?*

Preface

Before kindling Hanukkah lights, we recite a blessing that expresses our fulfillment of a commandment that God Himself bestowed upon us: "Who has sanctified us with His commandments and instructed us [*asher kiddeshanu be-mitzvotav, ve-tzivvanu*] to kindle the Hanukkah light."

Where in God's Law does such a commandment appear?

Sa'adiah Gaon and *Ta'Amei Ha-Mitzvot*

This chapter follows Sa'adiah Gaon (889–942) into a dimension of the study of the *taryag mitzvot*, the ostensible 613 Torah-mandated commandments,[1] assessing his claim that kindling Hanukkah lights is a Torah requirement (*d'orayta*) and not just a rabbinic one (*d'rabbanan*). We will draw upon his biblical commentaries as well as several sources, including the *Ba'al Halakhot Gedolot*,[2] the Book of Com-

---

1. On Sa'adiah's counting of mitzvoth, see further in the chapter on the *Azharot*.
2. The *Halakhot Gedolot* – often abbreviated as *Bahag* – is a compendium of talmudic and early geonic law that was composed in approximately the ninth century CE. It reflects primarily Babylonian jurisprudence with only a limited influence of Palestinian law and custom, and it is generally attributed to a scholar named Shim'on Qayara. The list of 613 commandments, to which

mandments (*Sefer ha-Mitzvot*) of Maimonides, and the criticisms of Nahmanides.

In the process, we will discuss the perameters of the disagreement over Torah ordained commandments vs. those that are rabbinically ordained, and see how the struggle with the Karaites prompted Sa'adiah to propose a novel and ingenious solution to the problem posed by Hanukkah.[3]

Background

Two excerpts from the Gemara form the background for this discussion:

> Rabbi Simlai expounded: 613 commandments were given to Moses-365 prohibitions, as the number of days in a solar year and 248 positive [commandments], as the number of limbs in a human body. Rav Hamnuna said: The verse says, "Torah was commanded us by Moses" (Deuteronomy 33:4). The numerical value of Torah is 611, [plus] "I am [the Lord your God]" and "You shall not have...," which we heard directly from God, [equal] 613 (*Makkot* 23b–24a).
>
> Which [blessing] is recited? "Who has sanctified us with His [commandments] and commanded us to kindle the Hanukkah light." And where did He so command us? R. Avya said, in the verse: "Do not stray [*lo tasur*]... from the word that they declare to you" (Deut. 17:11). R. Nehemiah said, in the verse: "Ask your father and let him tell you, and your grandfather, who will explain it" (Deut. 32:7).(Shabbat 23a)

By assigning the same blessing formula ("who has sanctified us...") to Hanukkah lights as they had to *tzitzit*, *tefillin*, and *b'rit milah* (circum-

---

Maimonides took such exception, appears in the introduction, whose relationship to the body of the work is disputed.

3. Cf. Moshe Zucker, in *Proceedings of the American Academy for Jewish Research*, vol. 49 (1982).

cision), the talmudic sages treated Hanukkah as a *d'oraita* commandment, too. The inquiry we shall present here deals with the question posed in the second talmudic statement: *ve-heikhan tzivvanu*; namely, from which verse in the Torah does this mitzvah derive?

Maimonides' Position

In his brief preface to each new topic in the *Mishneh Torah*, Maimonides noted the number of *mitzvot* included in that general topic, dividing them into directives (*'aseih*) and prohibitions (*lo ta'aseh*), and then specified each one individually. For instance, *Hilkhot Yesodei ha-Torah*, the first topic in the very first book (*Sefer ha-Madda'*), consists of 10 *mitzvot* – 6 *'aseih* and 4 *lo ta'aseh*. *Hilkhot Keri'at Sh'ma'*, which begins book two (*Seifer ha-Ahavah*), consists of a single mitzvah, and *Hilkhot Shabbat*, at the beginning of book three (*Seifer Zemanim*), consists of 5 *mitzvot*: 2 *'aseih* and 5 *lo ta'aseh*.

At the beginning of *Hilkhot Megillah ve-Chanukkah*, Maimonides wrote:

> They consist of two positive commandments of rabbinic origin, which are not to be included in the total of 613.

In the introduction to his *Seifer ha-Mitzvot*, however, he goes into greater detail regarding both *neir Chanukkah* and the Megillah.[4]

> The first rule is that we shall not include in this total any [*mitzvot*] of rabbinic origin. This matter should not have had to be mentioned since it appears to be so obvious. If the Talmud says: "613 [*mitzvot*] were commanded to Moses at Sinai," how can anything of rabbinic origin be included?
>
> We have made this observation, nevertheless, since some

---

4. Maimonides's *Seifer ha-Mitzvot*, *Guide for the Perplexed*, *Peirush ha-Mishnayyot*, and most of his epistles and responsa were written in Arabic. The text we translate here into English is that of Rav Yosef Kafih in his edition of *Seifer ha-Mitzvot* published by Mosad haRav Kook (Jerusalem, 1958).

have already erred and included *neir Chanukkah* and reading the Megillah among the 613 commandments, along with the daily recitation of 100 *berakhot*, comforting mourners, visiting the sick, burying the dead, clothing the naked, calculating the seasons, and the eighteen occasions on which Halleil is completed.

It is incredible that anyone reading the [Talmudic] text: "...were commanded to Moses at Sinai," could think to include the recitation of Halleil – which was David's own praise to God – as though Moses had been commanded about it, or the kindling of the neir Chanukkah – which was instituted by the Sages during the Second Temple – or the reading of the Megillah.

I do not think it could really occur to anyone that Moses was told at Sinai to command us that if something occurred between ourselves and the Greeks at the close of the period of our independence, that we should kindle a *neir Chanukkah*.

...The rule is: If we were to count every positive and negative rabbinic commandment, the total number [of commandments] would run into the thousands. This is patently obvious; namely, that nothing of rabbinic origin can be included in the 613 commandments, since that number refers strictly to the Torah and includes nothing of rabbinic origin. The fact that there are other people who arbitrarily list some rabbinic commandments – while omitting others – is entirely unacceptable, whoever they may be. We have already explained this and documented it so that no doubt should remain.

The Loyal Opposition

Who were the Sages who presumed – erroneously, according to Maimonides – to count "obvious" rabbinic enactments side by side with genuine Torah commandments?

The approach that Maimonides criticized in *Seifer ha-Mitzvot* is usually identified with the *Halakhot Gedolot*. This identification is made explicit by Nahmanides in his annotations on *Seifer ha-Mitzvot*:

> In the first principle of this essay, the great rabbi, o.b.m., criticizes the *Ba'al Halakhot Gedolot*, o.b.m., because the latter, in his enumeration of the commandments, had included the reading of the Megillah and the kindling of the Hanukkah lights... while all these are actually rabbinic prescriptions and are not from the Torah. His [Maimonides's] criticisms here are extremely telling, and nearly convincing.

Nahmanides' Reservations

Why did Nahmanides refer to Maimonides' critique of the Bahag's position as "nearly convincing"? Can it really be defended?

Nahmanides, in that same critique, put up a spirited and detailed defense of this position based upon his analysis of the passage cited from *Makkot* 23b, where the number of 613 commandments is introduced:

1. Why assume, he asked, that Rabbi Simlai's homily represents the unanimous opinion of the Sages? Perhaps it represents only his individual opinion and there is room to disagree with it?

   After all, he explained, it often happens in the Gemara that two sages disagree regarding the force of a particular verse with one saying it is obligatory (*chovah*) and the other saying it is only optional (*reshut*). If we assume the number 613 to be absolute, however, then whoever says that a particular Torah injunction is only optional, falls short of 613 by one commandment, and he must find another commandment to replace it. Now each of them can list 613 commandments, but between the two of them the list numbers more than 613 different commandments, since each one counts as mandatory something which the other feels is only optional.

   If we were to make a list of all such disagreements, he noted, we would realize that there is the potential in the Talmud for many more biblical commandments than the 613 we customarily list.

2. Even the alpha-numerical allusions (*gematriyot*) provided in support of the number 613 (such as that of Rav Hamnuna in the passage cited above) are not unanimous opinions. For example, the Midrash Tanchuma (quoted by Rashi to Numbers 15:39) states that *tzitzit* are reminders of the *taryag mitzvot* on account of a *gematriya*: *tzitzit* = 600, plus 8 strings and 5 knots = 613. And yet, Nahmanides pointed out that Beit Hillel required only three strings, and only the uppermost knot is biblically required.

3. Moreover, it seems that the *Bahag* had a different text of that talmudic passage, which, while close to our own, is not entirely identical with it. While we read: "613 commandments were given to Moses," and Maimonides read: "Were spoken to Moses at Sinai," our text of the *Bahag* (ed. Hildesheimer, p. 9) reads: "That Israel received at Sinai (*shekib'lu Yisra'el*)." Nahmanides cited it as: "Israel was commanded (*nitztavvu Yisra'el*)," which is broad enough to accommodate any commandments we have been practicing regularly.[5]

4. Finally, Nahmanides argued, even if we accept the figure of 613 biblical commandments, the phrase "given to Moses" is not to be taken literally, since many commandments that are indisputably biblical were not revealed to Moses, but to Aaron. And if the conclusion of this passage is not to be taken literally regarding the authors of the commandments, then why should the opening, which stipulates their amount?

---

5. Nahmanides uses the phrase, "the commandments that were customary among Israel throughout the generations (*hanohagot beYisra'el ledorot*)," without regard to where, and by whom, they were commanded.

Sa'adiah and Hanukkah

If Maimonides's objection to the inclusion of Hanukkah among the biblical commandments is based on his rejection of "do not stray" (*lo tasur*) as a catchall for rabbinic commandments, then why was it necessary for him to add the specific argument of "[could it really] occur to anyone that Moses, at Sinai, was told to command us" regarding an episode that would not occur for over 1,000 years? The catchall of *lo tasur* was not the only Torah basis the medievals found for the commandment of *neir Chanukkah*. Sa'adiah Gaon, in particular, used great ingenuity in discovering another verse from which that commandment derived.

Sa'adiah, who was the Gaon (dean) of the Sura yeshiva of Baghdad in the second quarter of the tenth century, was locked in a mortal struggle with the Karaites over the validity and authority of the Oral Law. The Karaites argued for a nearly literal interpretation of the Torah, while he championed the Sages as its only reliable interpreters, and the rabbinic tradition (*torah she-be'al peh*) as the only valid record of that interpretation. In accordance with this position, he imposed two conditions on every biblical exegete:

> His interpretations must conform with that which is written in "the first prophecy," namely the Torah of Moses, for it is the central pivot around which the words of all the prophets revolve, and all ambiguities are to be resolved by analogy to it.
>
> Secondly, his interpretations may not contradict the [oral] tradition of the prophets, or the received tradition of our ancestors, for they are the criteria by which all thoughts must be measured, and the test of every way of belief.
>
> (Introduction to the Torah)

In his own commentaries, Sa'adiah strove to demonstrate the complete identity of rabbinic law and the biblical text, as well as to impart a legal value to the narrative portions of the Torah, in order to refute the Karaites. It is in the context of his struggle to assert rabbinic supremacy that he sought to establish the Torah origins of even Hanukkah and Purim, in order to refute the Karaites' accusation that Rabbinic Judaism was, in their words, a "man-made" religion, formulated arbitrarily by the Sages of the Talmud without scriptural authority.

Thus, he wrote in his own *Seifer ha-Mitzvot*:

> It is included in [scriptural] tradition that the day on which He shall deliver us from the descendants of Amalek shall be proclaimed a festival, as it is written: "Write this, as a remembrance, in the book" (Exodus 17:14). And when God shall grant the Levites a military victory over their enemies, they shall designate that time [as a festival], as it is written: "May God bless his troops and accept the deeds of his hands" (Deuteronomy 33:11).

The Missing Link

How did Sa'adiah discover a reference to Hanukkah in Moses's blessing to the tribe of Levi? (While the same can be asked about the Megillah, the connection between Purim and Amalek is much more obvious and does not appear to be as much of a "forced" interpretation.) He explained this in his commentary on Daniel, chapter 2:

> When I reviewed the entire written and oral tradition to find a story about a military victory by the tribe of Levi, I found only one such reference, namely to the era of the Greeks. This is the national tradition regarding the five sons of Mattathias, called the Hasmoneans, who fought against one of the Greek kings named Antiochus, and whose victory established their rule for 260 years.
>
> This is what Moses prophesied about them previously [referring to the verse (Deuteronomy 33:11) that we cited] and the proof is that he made specific reference to the "loins" (*motnayim*), because the kingdom of the Greeks is identified with the loins [of the statue] in the dream of Nebuchadnezzar (Daniel 2:32 ff.).

It seems likely, then, that while Maimonides's general objection to the inclusion of non-Torah commandments among the essential 613 commandments is aimed at the *Bahag*, his criticism of the attempt to put *neir Chanukkah* on the biblical list is aimed specifically at Saʻadiah.

Conclusion

The disagreement between Maimonides and Saʻadiah is not without analogy today. We, like Saʻadiah, are often hard-pressed by elements within the Jewish community to account for our equal observance of "merely" rabbinic injunctions alongside "genuine" Torah laws. We, too, are frequently challenged to defend rabbinic enactments against the charge that they are arbitrary, discriminatory, and without scriptural authority. The positions of Maimonides, Nahmanides, the *Bahag*, and Saʻadiah, offer us alternative paradigms of response.

Like the *Bahag* – according to the explanation of Nahmanides – we may opt for the defense of "tradition." Once any custom survives the test of time and becomes an inseparable part of Jewish practice and commitment, then arguments over its legal ancestry are superfluous. Or we may choose, like Saʻadiah, to enter into rationalistic textual combat in defense of rabbinic authority and attempt to persuade our opponents of the precise Torah origin of even acknowledged rabbinic decrees.

A third path would have us, like Maimonides, reject the way of the *Bahag* as blurring necessary distinctions between the biblical and the rabbinic and that of Saʻadiah as apologetic. Rather, we can select the position that many laws are, unabashedly, rabbinic in origin, for to disguise this fact is to impugn the essence of rabbinic authority, and if the "Karaites" (or the naysayers of today) will not light *neir Chanukkah* entirely on the authority of the Sages, then linking the commandment to a Torah verse is not likely to change their established patterns of thought and behavior.

Waging War on Shabbat
The Legacy of the Hasmoneans

Preface
In this chapter, we will discuss the halakhic-historical issue regarding the permissibility of, or prohibition against, waging war on Shabbat.

Background
To put this issue into historical context, we must go back to the beginning of the Second Temple era. Ezra and Nehemiah found that the laws of Shabbat (along with those of intermarriage and Jewish slavery) were being regularly violated. Along with their successors – known, collectively, as the "Men of the Grand Assembly" (*Anshei Keneset haGedolah*)[1] – they took the initiative to regain widespread observance of Shabbat through a series of enactments (*takkanot*). The result of their combined efforts was a stronger and longer lasting practice of Shabbat, and of many other commandments, throughout the duration of the Second Temple period. (Remember: When the Sages cast about for a cause of the destruction of the Second Temple, they blamed it on gratuitous enmity (*sin'at chinam*) rather than on the failure to keep

---

1. There is consensus that this term refers to the governing body of the Jewish people in the Land of Israel during the Persian period of the Second Temple. However, on account of a 165-year discrepancy between rabbinic and general historical chronology of this period, the question of the identities of the individual members of the Assembly – indeed, the question of whether it had 120 members at all times, or 120 in total, is still in dispute.

ritual observances.) Indeed, they were so successful in instilling the spirit of Shabbat observance that the people appear to have taken it to a near-fatal excess during the Hellenistic and Roman periods by refusing to take up arms on Shabbat even in their own defense.

Introduction to the Sources

The two principal sources of our historical information about this era, the Books of the Maccabees and the works of Josephus Flavius, deserve an introduction.

a. The Books of the Maccabees (there are two) are part of the "Apocrypha," books that were written by Jews during the Hellenistic period. Some of these books, like that of Ben Sira, were written in Hebrew, and were well-regarded by the Sages.[2] Others, including the Books of the Maccabees, were written in Greek, Book One by authors whose motives were suspect due to their political or sectarian bias, and Book Two by responsible authors.

b. Josephus Flavius was a Jewish general during the war against Rome. He wrote (in Greek) a history of the Jewish people (*Jewish Antiquities*), an account of the war (*Wars of the Jews*), and an autobiography. Although he was an aristocrat, and a kohen, he eventually switched sides to join the Romans, and his works are often treated with skepticism.

The Contrast

Juxtapose the following passages to observe the strikingly different attitudes towards Shabbat that they exemplify.

> At that time I saw, in Judea, people threshing on Shabbat, bringing the bundles on their donkeys – including grapes and figs

---

2. In about half a dozen places, the Talmud quotes passages from Ben Sira as though they were scriptural, and declares that "worthwhile matters" therein may be taught (*Sanhedrin* 100b) without violating the ban on reading extraneous books (*sefarim chitzonim*).

and other baggage – and transporting them to Jerusalem on Shabbat (Nehemiah 13:15–16).

The [Greeks] arose, suddenly, to fall upon them on Shabbat, saying to them: How long will you refuse to obey the king? And the men in their midst did not raise their hands to hurl a stone or to silence them... and [the Greeks] fell upon them on Shabbat and killed all those in the cave... about 1,000 people (1 Maccabees 2:29–37).

Having deduced the different attitudes towards Shabbat exemplified by these two texts, the question is: What brought about such a radical change in the attitude towards the sanctity of Shabbat and its observance?

The answer, as we have already indicated, is the enactments of the Men of the Grand Assembly. While there are several references in the Talmud to the accomplishments of Ezra, Nehemiah, and the Assemblymen (see *Baba Kamma* 82a), we cite, here, a passage from the laws of Shabbat in Maimonides:

> The Sages prohibited carrying some things on Shabbat in the manner of the weekday... so that the day of Shabbat will not appear ordinary (*Shabbat* 24:12).[3]

These enactments, then, regulated even such mundane activities as carrying. Being forced to consider how their behavior on Shabbat differed from that of every other day, people were alerted to the special nature of Shabbat. Gradually, however, they became so sensitive that they appear to have placed Shabbat observance even above the preservation of life. That, as later events would show, was a disaster; the enemies of the Jews took advantage of the situation and timed their attacks for the Sabbath day.

---

3. The Ra'avad, in his gloss on Maimonides (24:13), associated this prohibition expressly with Nehemiah (cf. Nehemiah 13: 15 ff.).

The Maccabean Response

The deaths of 1,000 Jewish men, women, and children (described in the text of 1 Maccabees 2, cited above) prompted Mattathias and the Hasmoneans to respond by countering future attacks on Shabbat with a defensive battle:

> They said to one another: If we all act as our brothers have, and refuse to defend our lives and beliefs, we will shortly be destroyed. They decided on that day: Whosoever will attack us on Shabbat, we will fight back; we will not die like our brothers in the caves[4] (1 Maccabees 2:38–41).

Indeed, when the Syrian general Bacchides attacked Jonathan the Hasmonean on Shabbat, Jonathan rallied his soldiers, saying: "Let us defend ourselves ... we are under attack both front and rear and there is no place else to turn" (1 Maccabees 9:43–45).

The Halakhic Response: Defensive Measures

While the Jews now responded to attacks on Shabbat, they still refrained from addressing less imminent threats. The Syrian general Nicanor attempted to surprise the Maccabees by an attack on Shabbat (2 Maccabees 15:1–5), since the Jewish defenders would not arm themselves on Shabbat until they actually came under attack. He failed only because he lost the element of surprise long enough to enable the Jews to reach their weapons.

This inspired a reformulation of the law:

> If Gentiles attacked Jewish cities, they are to be met by force of arms even if it entails profaning Shabbat. In what circumstances? If they are intent upon murder.... Originally people would store their arms in a house adjacent to the city wall. Once

---

4. Josephus's version of this story, reported in his *Antiquities* (12.6.2), adds: "This law is in force to this very day. If need be, we are permitted to fight, even on Shabbat."

upon a time, however, they were attacked, and were rushing to secure their arms, and ended up killing each other [even more than the enemy killed]. They then made a ruling that everyone should store his own weapons at home.... (Tosefta, *Eruvin* 3:5–6)

The permission to wage a defensive battle on Shabbat hearkens back to the time of Mattathias and the Hasmoneans. While it was permissible to fight back, it was not permissible to bear arms before an attack was launched; rather the arms were stored in a central armory. The change in the law reflected the consequences of the attack by Nicanor. In any event, only defensive postures were permitted. Preemptive strikes against the enemy, even one whose bellicose intentions were obvious, were still prohibited.

After the Roman general Pompei built a siege ramp to assault Jerusalem, Josephus wrote:

Had we not been accustomed, from the days of yore, to rest on Shabbat, that ramp would never have been completed.... Even though the law permits us to protect ourselves against attacks, it still does not permit us to engage our enemies when they are not [directly attacking] (*Antiquities* 14.4.2–3).

Offensive Measures

Later, the *halakhah* was expanded to permit offensive strikes as well:

An army embarking on an optional war may not besiege a Gentile city less than three days before Shabbat. Once they started the siege, however, they may not interrupt it even for Shabbat. This was the way Hillel, the Elder, interpreted the verse "until it falls" (Deut. 20:20) to include even Shabbat. (Tosefta, *Eruvin* 4:7)[5]

---

5. Several manuscripts of the Tosefta read "Shammai, the Elder" rather than

The War Against Rome

When King Agrippa II, in 66 CE, appealed to the Judeans to cease their rebellion against Rome, he told the Jews, in essence, that on account of Shabbat they would fail whichever way they turned. As Josephus recounted:

> If you keep the Shabbat laws and do no work, you will easily fall into the hands of your enemies just as your ancestors did at the time of Pompei who strengthened his siegeworks on their days of rest. And if you opt to violate the Torah laws by fighting on Shabbat, you will lose all purpose for the battle you are conducting, since your entire purpose is not to transgress even the slightest law of your ancestors. How will you call upon God to do battle for you if you deliberately violate His ritual laws? (Wars 2.16.4)

These words, which have all the earmarks of demagoguery, are belied by the record of the war against Rome in which battles were regularly fought on Shabbat. Time after time Josephus reported on Jewish military actions on Shabbat (cf. *Wars* 2.17.10), and even when he reported on the slaughter of the Jews of Caesaria by their Gentile neighbors on Shabbat (*Wars* 2.18.1 ff.), he noted that they were killed "before they were able to defend themselves," implying that if they

---

Hillel. This reading is upheld by parallel passages in the Talmud (*Shabbat* 19a), *Sifrei Devarim* (203–4) and the *Midrash ha-Gadol*, and appears to be more correct. Further analysis of the Tosefta – based upon *Midrash ha-Gadol* – shows that Shammai ruled only that if a siege was begun three days before Shabbat it need not be abandoned on Shabbat; it was a later Tanna, R. Yoshiya (of the period of Yavneh), who extended the ruling further and, based upon the verse cited, declared that such a siege could even be initiated on Shabbat (cf. Yerushalmi *Shabbat* 1:8, re: Jericho). Shammai's ruling appears to have been designed to standardize the various practices that had been in force since the time of the Hasmonean King Alexander Yannai who, for 15 years (between 103–76 BCE), extended the boundaries of the Jewish kingdom to include, specifically, all the pagan cities (*'ir shel goyim*) in Palestine.

had had the opportunity to defend themselves they would not have let Shabbat stand in the way.

He likewise reported the following when the Jews of Jerusalem were attacked on Sukkot:

> They abandoned their holiday and took up their weapons. Relying upon their superior numbers, they sallied forth from the city with war cries – without order or a plan of battle – paying no attention to the sanctity of the Sabbath even though they were accustomed to accord that day the greatest sanctity (*Wars* 2.19.2).

He even added: "The intense anger which drew the Jews' attention away from their sacred rituals, gave them added strength and determination to fight."

T'was the Night Before Christmas: A Look at "Nittel-Nacht"

Preface: Jews and Gentiles

To deliberately refrain from Torah study is uncharacteristic behavior for any religious Jew, let alone for people of piety and devotion. And yet, that is precisely what many of the pious and devoted regularly do twice each year: on Tish'ah b'Av and on Christmas Eve. The study of Torah is an invariable source of joy, and abstinence therefrom is a visible sign of mourning. As such, it is prohibited on Tish'ah B'Av as well as on occasions of personal bereavement. Refraining from Torah study on Christmas Eve, however, has a far more complicated – even labyrinthine – history.

The Mishnah prohibited trade between Jews and Gentiles on Gentile festivals out of concern lest the Gentile celebrate his commercial success through spending money on his worship, making the Jew an inadvertent accessory to idolatry. In the twelfth and thirteenth centuries, however, Ashkenazi scholars amended the talmudic legislation to meet the needs of their society by distinguishing between contemporary Christians and the idolaters of yore.[1] Yet even under these relaxed restrictions, trade on Christmas Eve (and on Easter) remained prohibited. Indeed, one of the earliest explicit references to Christmas as "Nittel"[2] occurs in a responsum of Rabbi Israel Isserlein

---

1. See Jacob Katz: *Exclusiveness and Tolerance* (Oxford, 1961), Chapter 1.
2. The etymology of *Nittel* is moot. Some see its origin in the Latin for "birth"

(Austria; 1390–1460) that includes a restriction on social contacts with Christians on the eighth day of Christmas, i.e., New Year's Day.

Torah Study on Christmas

The custom of foregoing Torah study on Christmas Eve is unattested to before the fifteenth century and, since its appearance, has frequently been challenged. The *Chatam Sofeir* (Rabbi Moses Sofer of Pressburg, 1762–1839), for instance, expressed skepticism over the practice. He recommended going to sleep early, waking at midnight, and then resuming a full course of study. He also noted a practice of keeping the ritual bath (*mikveh*) closed that night and explicitly called it a foolish custom (*minhag sh'tut*). Other sources (cited in the general literature on laws and customs) viewed it as a preventive measure, intended to keep Jews off the streets and thereby protect them against anti-Semitic excesses that were anticipated on that night. As reasonable a motive as this might seem, however, synagogue prayer on Christmas Eve was never abolished although it surely put Jews in harm's way.

While the custom appears to be rooted in the Ashkenazi Jewish historical experience (and is absent in Sephardi sources), not all Ashkenazim viewed it alike. Hasidim have tended to be more punctilious in its observance – some Hasidic rebbes would neither study nor receive requests from their Hasidim before midnight – whereas the Lithuanian academies (*yeshivot*) declined to interrupt their customary Torah studies. Indeed, their deans (*rashei yeshivah*) were outspoken in their opposition to the abstention from Torah study on any grounds (some would say in deliberate reproach to the Hasidim). There were

---

(abbreviated from *natali domini*, "birth of the Lord") and related to the more familiar word "nativity." Others derive it from a Semitic root that yields either "the one who was taken" (ניטל) or "the one who was hung" (נתלה) depending on whether it is spelled with a Hebrew *tet* or *tav*. In either case, it appears to be a euphemism for Jesus that was adopted either out of a religious concern – to shun explicit reference to an alien deity – or, as a practical measure, to avoid Christian censorship.

also distinctions between those living among Roman Catholics, who observe Christmas on December 25, and those in Slavic lands, where Orthodox Christmas is observed on January 7.[3]

Neither of those two dates, of course, carries any significance according to the Jewish calendar, a fact that has led to considerable speculation concerning a public fast day (*ta'anit tzibbur*) prescribed by the *Shulchan Arukh* for the ninth of Tevet for no express reason (*Orach Chayyim* 580:2). Based upon the calculations of a twelfth-century rabbi and astronomer, Abraham bar Hiyya, it has been conjectured that this date marks Jesus's Jewish birthday. Some have even suggested that "Nittel" stands for *nolad yeishu tet l'tevet* (Jesus was born on the ninth of Tevet).

That religious authorities would have ordered a public fast day to mark the occasion of Jesus's birth is a sign of their consternation over the long-term impact of Christianity on the Jewish people; that they obscured the reason for it is a sign of their circumspection. A popular explanation for customs observed on "Nittel" links them to occult, Kabbalistic notions of essential evil (*kelippot*), and its proliferation on Jesus's birthday.

If Not Torah, Then What?

To those Jews who abjured public Torah study on Christmas Eve, the question naturally arose: What to do instead? To many, the answer was simplicity itself: Study Torah at home! To others, who may either have misapprehended the nature of the prohibition or were, in any event, seeking a reprieve from study, another answer was: Play cards! It may be only a coincidence that this pastime was first noted among Jews in 1415, around the time that "Nittel" was first mentioned, but,

---

3. This inconsistency is due to the discrepancy between the Julian ands Gregorian calendars discussed in an earlier chapter (see "The 5th of December"). Because the newer calendar was introduced at the initiative of the Roman Catholic Church, it was rejected by the Orthodox Church.

once introduced, it, like other games of chance, cast an addictive spell over European Jewry. Numerous communal attempts to ban the practice altogether succeeded only in abating it, with exemptions formally granted on minor festive occasions including Rosh Hodesh, Hanukkah, and Purim. It was also specifically sanctioned on Christmas (curiously paralleling the practice of otherwise temperate Christians at Cambridge University in the time of John Milton).

Alternatives to card playing include chess, and the proximity of Christmas Eve to Hanukkah suggests that *dreidel* play may have been invented to pass the time on "Nittel." Indeed, a gambling game with a spinning top (called a teetotum), first mentioned in the sixteenth century, was popular in Europe at Christmastime. More unusual is the custom of reading Toledot Yeishu, a medieval Jewish version of the Life of Jesus, and even more unusual – to the point of being nearly apocryphal – is the custom to spend the evening tearing toilet paper for use throughout the year on Shabbat and festivals when tearing is prohibited. Practice of such customs varies widely today.

Tu BiSh'vat
From "New Year" to "Arbor Day"

Preface
Nogah Hareuveni, the Israeli botanist and naturalist who established the biblical and mishnaic agricultural park Neot Kedumim, labeled the holiday of Tu biSh'vat, "a festival of the Land of Israel that was developed in the Diaspora."[1]

What are the classical origins and significance of Tu biSh'vat, and when and why was it incorporated into the calendar as the Jewish "Arbor Day"?

The Origin of the Occasion
Sh'vat is the eleventh month of the Jewish year when the count begins with Nisan. The name Sh'vat (from the same root as *shevet*, meaning a staff or club) was introduced at the time of the return from the Babylonian exile (sixth century BCE) and denotes the month of destructive rain. The earliest reference to the 15th of Sh'vat (the Hebrew letters *tet* and *vav*, spelling *tu*, are, numerically, 9 and 6, respectively) appears in the opening Mishnah of the tractate Rosh Hashanah:

> There are four [days that mark a] "New Year"... The first of Sh'vat marks the New Year for trees, according to the School of Shammai, while according to the School of Hillel it occurs on the fifteenth of the month.

---
1. Nogah Hareuveni: *Nature in Our Biblical Heritage* (Neot Kedumim, 1980).

Since the ruling here follows the School of Hillel, the Gemara includes the following clarification:

> The Rabbis said: A tree that began to bear fruit before the 15th of Sh'vat is tithed according to the previous year. After the 15th of Sh'vat, it is tithed according to the following year. (*Rosh Hashanah* 15b)

The rabbinic concept of a "New Year" indicates a point in time at which accounts are due or settled. The concept of Rosh Hashanah (1 Tishrei) as a "day of judgment" also fits this definition. Another such accounting concerns the tithe that had to be paid on agricultural produce. Just as American taxes are assessed on income earned up to a specific point in time (i.e., December 31), a date needed to be established to determine whether produce would be tithed on the account of the preceding year or the subsequent one.

The choice of 15 Sh'vat as the cut-off point is explained by the Talmud (*Rosh Hashanah* 14a) on grounds of weather and climate: "since most of the year's rain has fallen, although most of the [winter] season[2] has yet to occur."

---

2. Yair Goldreich: "When Have 'Most of the Rains Passed?' Setting the Date of the New Year for Trees," Bar-Ilan University (5762). http://www.biu.ac.il/JH/Parasha/eng/beshalah/gol.html:

> The season referred to is that of Tevet or winter, extending from the shortest day (December 21) to the spring equinox (March 21). Since the Talmud uses the term "season" (Heb. *tekufah*), and the seasons are based on the solar calendar, we must translate the Hebrew date, based on a lunar calendar, to the date used in the secular solar-based calendar.
>
> If we take the average secular dates that correspond to the first and fifteenth of Sh'vat, we come up with the dates of January 16 and 30, respectively. The earliest these Hebrew dates fall with respect to the recent secular calendar is the 2nd and 16th of January (in 1995), and the latest (in 1987), January 31 and February 14, respectively. In other words, there is a maximal difference of one month. Taking the median dates instead of the average dates yields the same results in the secular calendar.

Rashi (ad. loc.) explained:

Most of the year's rain has fallen: Most of the days of the rainy season have elapsed, this being the time of the early rains[3] when the sap appears in trees, and the fruits begin to ripen. Since most of the Teiveit [winter] season has yet to occur and the time of ripening fruit has not arrived, the "New Year" should have been fixed in Adar.

Rain and the Land of Israel

In describing the Land of Israel to the Jewish people, Moses attributed existential significance to rain:

The land you are about to enter and settle is unlike the land of Egypt you have left, in which one could sow seeds and irrigate by foot [i.e., by digging a trench for the Nile water with your foot], like a vegetable garden. The land you are going to settle is a land of mountains and valleys, which absorbs water as rain from heaven. It is a land that the Lord, your God, inquires of perpetually; His eyes are upon it from the start of the year until its close. (Deuteronomy 11: 10–12)

Unlike Egypt, which is irrigated by the overflow of the Nile, the Land of Israel was totally dependent on rainfall, a resource not always available in sufficient quantity. This situation has not changed to this very day, as disagreements between Israel and her neighbors about water rights and usage testify.[4]

---

3. Prof. Goldreich explained:

   Talmudic literature speaks of the rainy season having three periods of *revi'ah* or initial rainfall moistening the parched soil and making it arable. The first *revi'ah* is approximately the first two weeks of Cheshvan, the second is the third week of Cheshvan, and third is the last week of Cheshvan or the beginning of Kisleiv (Ibid.).

4. With the advent of desalination of sea water, Israel's dependence on rain-

This is further complicated by the Torah's assertion that rainfall is not merely the product of auspicious meteorological conditions, but a function of the relationship between Israel and God as measured by the observance of Torah and *mitzvot*:

> If you follow My statutes and observe and perform My commandments, I shall grant your rains in their assigned times; the earth will yield its produce and trees will bear fruit (Leviticus 26:3–4).

And, on the other hand:

> If you do not obey Me and do not follow these commandments... I shall break your haughtiness; I shall make your heavens like iron and your land like bronze. You will wear yourselves out; your land will not yield its produce and the trees will not bear their fruit. (Leviticus 26: 14, 19–20)

So vital, indeed, is water to the maintenance of life that prayers were recited about water (Psalms 65:10–11, 2 Chronicles 6:26), kings were crowned alongside water (1 Kings 1:33–34), prophetic visions were granted there (Ezekiel 1:1), and public prayers recited there as well (Nehemiah 8:1–3).

The Turning Point of Winter

Returning to the Mishnah and the disagreement between the schools of Hillel and Shammai, we may ask: How did Tu bi-Sh'vat come to be identified as the point at which the winter rains had peaked? There are two answers: one scientific and the other speculative. We shall begin with the former.

---

water has become less consequential (see Seth M. Siegel: *Let There Be Water*, NY, 2015), in which case rain, in the texts quoted above, may be understood as a metaphor for God's sustenance, in general.

a. A responsum of R. Hayya Gaon (Baghdad; d. 1038) reveals an intimate knowledge of the climate of the Land of Israel:

> The fifteenth day of Sh'vat is the day that, in Arabic, is called "the second ember," on which fruit trees begin to absorb water and flourish.

According to Nogah Hareuveni, "embers" are heat waves associated with clusters of black, furry caterpillars that appear on wild vegetation and young wheat in the Land of Israel during the months of January and February. Based on accounts given by Arab villagers in the Galilee, he reported that they correspond to three successive warming trends that occur during the consecutive months of Tevet, Sh'vat, and Adar.

> The name "ember" was originally given not to the caterpillar but to an ember of heat that falls to earth from the heavens. In winter [so Arab folklore relates], the heat of summer turns into embers which hide between earth and the zodiac of heaven, leaving the cold to cover the earth.... The first ember is the "earth ember," to warm up the soil; the second is the "water ember," which heats up the water in the soil; the third is the "air ember," which heats up the air and forces the cold [to go] deep below ground.[5]

Beit Hillel regarded the middle trend, "the second ember," as the point at which the earth had warmed up enough to release water into the trees, so the fruiting process, from then on, belonged to the following year. Beit Shammai reasoned that the first trend was adequate to the task and that whatever water was drawn into the trees starting from 1 Sh'vat already belonged to the following year.

---

5. Hareuveni, *Nature* 107 ff., citing a 1935 article by Dr. Ephraim Hareuveni, his father.

b. The speculative answer rests upon the correspondence between 15 Sh'vat and 15 Av:

> Eliezer the Great said: From the fifteenth of Av onward, the strength of the sun wanes and trees were no longer cut down for the altar because they were no longer dry (*Ta'anit* 31a).

If the middle of Av marks the end of summer, then it is not unreasonable to assume that the middle of Sh'vat, exactly six months later, marks the end of winter.

How Tu Bi-Sh'vat Became "Arbor Day"

The Mishnah in Rosh Hashanah cited above declared 1 Tishrei to be the "New Year for planting trees," that is, the date that determines the age of a tree in respect of the laws of *'orlah* and *neta' reva'ai* that affect the consumption of fruit. As Nogah Hareuveni explained:

> Under normal circumstances, it would never occur to anyone in Israel to plant at the end of the hottest and driest part of the summer. Fixing the date for the new year for planting on the first of Tishrei ensured that the sapling would be a full three years old before it was permissible to eat of its fruit. Had the new year for planting been on Tu bi-Sh'vat, all those saplings that are normally planted in the rainy winter months of December and January would be considered one year old just one or two months later.[6]

Since most fruit trees, however, are deciduous and are usually planted, while still leafless, well before Tu bi-Sh'vat, how did Tu bi-Sh'vat become the "Arbor Day" of modern Israel?

Hareuveni attributed the practice to the early pioneers from Russia who were motivated (partly by Zionist education and partly by

---

6. *Op. cit.*, 188.

Socialist propaganda) to renew ancient agricultural traditions, and who associated them with the modern tradition that they remembered from home of eating fruit, preferably of the Land of Israel, on Tu bi-Sh'vat.

The "Jewish National Fund" (founded in 1901) institutionalized the practice by soliciting money for the explicit purpose of planting trees. Thus, was born the association of Tu bi-Sh'vat with "the little blue box," that has enabled the planting of over 250 million trees in Israel.[7]

The custom of eating fruit on Tu bi-Sh'vat appears to have begun in Germany and, by the sixteenth century, had spread to Eastern Europe and, later, to Western Europe and North Africa. It was intended to strengthen the longing for the days in which Israel dwelt securely in its home and could easily observe the commandments of tithes.

At about the same time, the Kabbalists of Safed, whose affinity to nature led them to go out to the fields to pray, began to mark the occasion with a festive meal paralleling the Passover seder. One of its key features, drinking four glasses of wine transitioning from white to red, was likely inspired by the physical changes that fruit trees in Israel undergo during this season.

---

7. The Jewish National Fund. https://www.jnf.org/our-work/forestry-green-innovations

Purim and Joseph
Design or Coincidence?

Preface

Here is a familiar story, minus the specific details. Whose story is it?

A young Jewish man is taken away from Eretz Yisrael by force and grows up in a foreign country. In spite of the difficulties, he perseveres and succeeds, but not without evoking a noticeable measure of jealousy and hostility (including what we today might call antisemitism). Eventually, he uses his abilities to provide the king with some lifesaving advice, and is rewarded by being appointed viceroy.

The king gives him his royal signet ring, symbolizing his high office, and has him dressed in royal garments. He is driven around on the royal horse and chariot, while a page goes before him, announcing his promotion and instructing the people to bow.

Now fully mature in years, the young man does not let all this go to his head. He remains a loyal Jew, faithful to God, and uses his position and influence for the benefit of the Jewish people.[1]

---

1. I might have added that a crucial episode in the young man's story occurs at night while someone was either asleep and dreaming, or unable to sleep, but that would have given it away.

Joseph and Mordechai: No Coincidence

While some of the details of our story may fit several historical personalities (including Shmuel ha-Nagid, Moses Montefiore, and Henry Kissinger), all the details are consistent with only two biblical personalities: Joseph and Mordechai.

For example, let us take the opening sentence, which describes our hero as someone taken forcibly from Eretz Yisrael. Joseph said of himself: "I was stolen out of the land of the Hebrews" (Genesis 40:15), and the Book of Esther states of Mordechai: "he was exiled from Jerusalem" (2:6).

The "life-saving advice," in the case of Joseph, refers to his grain storage program, while in Mordechai's case, it refers to the warning he gave Ahasuerus about Bigtan and Teresh.

Literary similarities exist between the Torah's narrative of Joseph and the Book of Esther as well. Joseph advised Pharaoh: "Appoint officers (*veyafkeid pekidim*)...who will gather up (*veyikbetzu*) [grain]" (Genesis 41:34–35), and Ahasuerus's consultants advised: "Let the king appoint officers (*veyafkeid hamelekh pekidim*)...who will gather up (*veyikbetzu*) [women]" (Esther 2:3). Judah, pleading before Joseph to spare Benjamin, lamented: "Lest I see the evil that will befall my father" (44:34), while Esther lamented before Ahasuerus: "Lest I see the evil that will befall my nation" (8:6).

There are far too many points of both actual and literary correspondence[2] to be dismissed as coincidence. It appears, rather, that the authors of Megillat Esther made a deliberate attempt to pattern their description of the story of Purim after that of Joseph. Why? What parallels did they see between them? What is it about Joseph that they wanted us to be reminded of when we read the story of Mordechai and Esther?

---

2. See Gavriel H. Cohen: *'Iyyunim bi-Megillat Esther* (Jerusalem: WZO, 1981).

Shared Themes

There appear to be four themes that are common to the two stories and their main characters:

a. Even a lone individual can play a crucial role in the history of the Jewish people, providing that individual is sufficiently devoted to his faith and his nation.
b. "History repeats itself." In its classical Jewish formulation: *ma'aseh 'avot siman la-banim* (i.e., parents' actions are signs for their children), or, in a beautiful passage from the Midrash Esther Rabbah (7:8): *baneha shel Rachel nisam shaveh, u-g'dulatam shavah*, "Rachel's children [Joseph and Mordechai] are alike in their miracles [perhaps: "trials"] and in their greatness."
c. The promise of redemption is inherent in every exile. Just as the refuge which Joseph provided his family in Egypt was followed by the Exodus and the haven which Esther provided for the Jews of Persia was followed by the return to Zion, so will each and every exile be followed by redemption and restoration in Eretz Yisrael.
d. Historical events which appear, on the surface, to be the results of ordinary human activities, or even of coincidence, are revealed – upon closer inspection – to be divinely ordained.

Coincidence or Design

Defining coincidence as "an episode or encounter not under the exclusive control of the principal characters," at which points do the Joseph or Purim stories appear to hinge upon a coincidence?

Can we agree that this, indeed, is not mere coincidence, and that there is a point when the accumulation of several sequential "coincidences" gives us pause to consider whether they are not, in fact, part of a plan?

Waxing somewhat literary, if "All the world's a stage, and all the men and women merely players," are we ad libbing our way through life, or,

JOSEPH: an Ishmaelite caravan passed by just as the brothers weakened in their resolve to kill Joseph; Joseph was already imprisoned in the cell into which Pharaoh's officers were subsequently thrown; his brothers' arrival in Egypt to purchase grain "happened" to come to Joseph's personal attention; etc.	PURIM: Ahashverosh peremptorily discarded Vashti, who was replaced by Esther, whose uncle, Mordechai, "happened" to uncover a plot to assassinate the king; that same Mordechai incured the wrath of Haman, whose plot to destroy the Jews could be thwarted only by Esther; etc.

unbeknownst to us, are we actually reading lines from a designated script?

Can the Fate of the Jewish People Ever Be Left Entirely to Chance?

It is our contention that even when minor, anonymous, characters appear to be acting of their own volition, they may really be carrying out a divinely ordained mission.

One of the most striking "coincidences" in the story of Joseph (following our prior definition of "coincidence") was his encounter, in a field outside Shechem, with "a man" who just "happened" to know the whereabouts of his brothers. Yet without this encounter, he would not, ostensibly, have fallen into his brothers' hands to be sold into Egyptian bondage.

Who was this anonymous man, and how "freely" did he fulfill his crucial role in this drama? Let us sample four outstanding medieval exegetes on this question: Rashi, Ibn Ezra, Rashbam, and Nahmanides.

"A man found him as he was lost in the field" (Gen. 37:15).

On the surface, this appears to be a typical exegetical falling-out. Rashi, basing himself upon the Midrash *Tanchuma*, identified "the

A. Rashi:	this was Gabriel
B. Ibn Ezra:	an ordinary passerby
C. Nahmanides:	a divinely ordained messenger

man" with "the man (actually the archangel) Gabriel" mentioned in Daniel 9:21. Ibn Ezra, adhering more strictly to the *peshat* of the verse, rejected Rashi's identification and wrote, matter-of-factly, that it was a chance passerby. Nahmanides, who often arbitrated between Rashi and Ibn Ezra, did so again, siding – as he most often did – with the former against the latter.

Once we introduce the commentary of Rashbam, however, the argument can take on a new complexion.

D. Rashbam:	This was written in praise of Joseph, who did not want to return to his father when he failed to find [his brothers] in Shechem; rather, he searched for them until he found them. Although he knew that they were jealous of him, he searched for them as his father had instructed.

Was Joseph – following Rashbam's interpretation – a "free agent"? Yes and no. On one hand, he could have stopped his search at any time and returned home; yet, on the other hand, the magnitude of his devotion to his father weighed so heavily upon him as to deprive him of much of his freedom of action in this regard.

Was "the man" who directed him – following this line of argument – a "free agent"? Likewise, yes and no. No one was forcing him to intercept Joseph and direct him to his brothers (and his fate); but what if "the man" was weighed down by an overriding obligation, similar to that of Joseph, which would render him as incapable (or unlikely) of declining his role in the play as Joseph was of declining his?

To whom, though, could the man have been so obliged? Rashi, Ibn

Ezra, and Nahmanides all answered: "To God!" Rather than disagreement among the exegetes, as we suggested at first, they are actually all in accord, and Nahmanides was harmonizing the positions of Rashi and Ibn Ezra, rather than choosing between them.

What, Nahmanides asked, do we call "a man" who, although surely mortal (Ibn Ezra), was acting out of the same immutable obligation towards God as that of Gabriel (Rashi)? He answered: an angel (*mal'akh*); an agent of God's purpose and design.[3]

---

3. See our elaboration on angels and their functions in the chapter above on "Angels Dancing on a Silicon Chip."

Korban Pesach
The Repudiation of Idolatry

Preface
The principal objective of this chapter is to explain the significance of the original paschal sacrifice (*korban Pesach*) as a repudiation of idolatry and a demonstration of complete faith in God. Along the way, we will also seek to clarify some of the laws of the sacrifice (as detailed in Exodus 12), as well as some passages in the Haggadah.

The Wicked Son: Why Is Exclusion an Act of Heresy?
In the Haggadah, the wicked son asks: "What is this ritual to you?" and the reply is: "[His use of the word] 'you' excludes himself. Since he has excluded himself from the general rule, he has rejected an essential [article of faith]."

Why is the refusal to participate in the paschal sacrifice regarded as a rejection of faith, an act of heresy? If someone fails to observe Shabbat, *kashrut*, or Yom ha-Kippurim, we do not necessarily declare them to be heretics; why is Pesach different? The answer comes from an analysis of one of the ten plagues.

After the plague of *'arov*,[1] Pharaoh offered to allow the Jews to bring sacrifices to God without leaving Egypt. Moses declined the offer, explaining:

---

1. Literally: "multitudes." Exegetes are divided on the question of whether they were multitudes of wild animals or, perhaps, of insects.

It would not be proper, because the Egyptians regard our sacrifices to the Lord as abominations. Could we break an Egyptian taboo [*to'avat mitzrayim*] before their very eyes without getting stoned? (Exodus 8:22).[2]

It appears, then, that to slaughter and eat the paschal lamb in public was to offer the gravest insult to the Egyptians and to their gods. Only those Israelites who were firmly committed to God and to Moses were prepared to take that risk. To participate under those circumstances was an instance of ultimate devotion. However, to refuse to participate meant that one was not convinced that God could really do all that He had promised, and that one still feared the Egyptians more than one feared God.

While a transgression of Shabbat or of *kashrut* is regrettable, it does not, per se, constitute either a denial of God or the recognition of some other power as greater than His. To reject the paschal sacrifice, however, was to reject monotheism in its struggle for recognition over the "abominations" of idolatry.

The self-exclusion of the wicked son from this ritual is tantamount to his refusal to disavow idolatry. The Haggadah's observation, "Were he there [in Egypt] he would not have been redeemed," is self-explanatory. By rejecting the paschal sacrifice and by honoring Egyptian abomination over divine commandment, he would have forfeited his right to redemption.[3]

---

2. We may recall that because the Egyptians held the eaters of the flesh of sheep and cattle in the lowest regard, Joseph's brothers were fed separately from the Egyptians (Gen. 43:32). Joseph also encouraged his brothers to list their occupations as shepherds in order to keep them isolated from the rest of Egypt (46:34). Both of these references feature the word abomination (*to'eivah*).

3. Recall that Rashi (Exodus 13:18) cited a (midrashic) opnion to the effect that fully 80% of the Jews enslaved in Egypt were not deserving of liberation and, ostensibly, died during the plague of darkness.

The Preparation of the *Korban Pesach* (Exodus 12)

QUESTION #1: THE PREAMBLE

Why was the 15th of Nisan chosen for the sacrifice?
Why was it necessary to select the sacrificial animal on the 10th day of Nisan?
Why was the blood smeared on the door-posts and lintel?

ANSWER:

The challenge of the paschal sacrifice, as we have just explained, was to see if the Jews would stake their lives on God and Moses and free themselves from their subservience to, and fear of, the Egyptians. Anything that increased the indignity to the Egyptians heightened the risk to the Jews and made the experience more meaningful.

Bearing this in mind, we can appreciate why 15 Nisan was chosen for the sacrifice. The astrological symbol of the month of Nisan is Aries, the ram, worshipped in Egypt as a deity, and the fifteenth day is the climax of a lunar month. The god of the Egyptians was to be slaughtered on the evening of the full moon of its very own month (ostensibly, the height of its own powers), and the Egyptians would be powerless to prevent it! By selecting the sheep or ram four days in advance of the actual sacrifice, the Jews were flaunting their intentions in the faces of their Egyptian neighbors, as though daring them to interfere.

Similarly, the requirement that the animal's blood be smeared on the door-posts and lintel was intended to force the Egyptians to suffer the further indignity of seeing its lifeblood, the essence of many pagan rituals, "profaned." While the Torah does not specifically say so, we assume that the blood was smeared on the outside of the doorposts and lintel to mark the house as a participant in the ritual and eligible, thereby, for protection from the plague that smote the firstborn. At that same time, it marked the house and its occupants as accomplices in the unfolding "heresy."[4]

---

4. If both door-posts and the lintel were smeared with blood, it is not farfetched to assume that the threshold was as well. Indeed, the Torah instructs

QUESTION #2: THE CONSUMPTION

> Why was it forbidden to eat the sacrifice raw?
> Why could it not be cooked in a pot but only roasted on an open flame?
> Why did it have to be roasted whole – with its head, hind parts, and internal organs, intact?

ANSWER:

These details were intended to increase the indignity the Egyptians were meant to suffer and, correspondingly, increase the risk to the Jews participating in the sacrifice.

Roasting the sheep (or ram), rather than cooking it in a pot or eating it raw, meant that the aroma could not be contained. Even if the Egyptians did not actually see their taboo being slaughtered, they could not avoid the smell. By requiring the limbs and principal organs to be kept intact, the identity of the roasting animal could not be denied.

A Jew who had slaughtered his lamb secretly, fearing Egyptian reprisals, could not easily disguise its subsequent preparation. His participation in the ritual of redemption had to be made public, one way or another.

These same points were made by the Tosafot commentary to the Torah, on the authority of Abraham Ibn Ezra:

> Since you are about to sacrifice an Egyptian abomination you might not think to roast it entirely, lest the Egyptians realize it. Therefore, it says... Since you might think to cook it in a closed pot, it says... And lest you think to cut off its head or legs so they cannot tell what it is, it says...

---

that the blood that was to be applied to the door-posts, etc., was to be taken by means of a bundle of hyssop from something called the *saf* (12:22). While Rashi (among others) identified it as a utensil, Ibn Ezra offered an interpretation that identifies it as the threshhold.

THE REPUDIATION OF IDOLATRY · 113

Participation in the Sacrificial Meal

QUESTION #1
Who is "an alien" (*ben neikhar*; 12:43) and why was he prohibited from partaking of the paschal sacrifice?

ANSWER:
Since the entire purpose of the paschal sacrifice was to force the Jews to overcome their fear of the Egyptians and declare their allegiance to God, it is obvious that non-Jews should not participate. Assuming, then, that the Torah is not merely stating the obvious, whom does it mean to exclude?

Targum Onkelos reflects this concern. He translated *ben neikhar* as *bar Yisra'el de-istallak*, "a Jew who has removed himself." This interpretation fits neatly into our own analysis of the "wicked son," who also "removed himself" from the paschal sacrifice. It is also reflected in Rashi's commentary: "one whose actions have alienated him from God."

QUESTION #2
Why is someone who is uncircumcised (*'areil*) forbidden to partake of the sacrifice (v. 48)?

ANSWER
Regarding the exclusion of the uncircumcised, we note that Joshua was commanded to circumcise all the Jews who were not circumcised in the desert before they could participate in the first paschal sacrifice to be celebrated in the Land of Israel (Joshua 5:2 ff.). One phrase that occurs there, and which duplicates a phrase we cited earlier, gives us a clue about the relationship of circumcision to the paschal sacrifice.

That phrase in Joshua (5:9) is: "Today, I [God] have removed the disgrace of Egypt (*cherpat Mitzrayim*) from upon you." On the analogy of "the abomination (*to'eivah*) of Egypt," which described their taboos of sacrificing or eating sheep (Gen. 43:32, 46:34, and Exodus 8:22), we have a reference here to the scorn that the Egyptians apparently heaped upon the Jewish ritual of circumcision.[5]

Because the paschal sacrifice symbolized total belief in God, someone who did not break completely with idolatry and its taboos was excluded from it. Similarly excluded was someone whose sensitivity to the scorn of idolaters prevented him from undergoing circumcision. If a Gentile slave or a resident alien (*geir toshav*) underwent circumcision, however, he became eligible to participate on an equal footing with a Jew (Exodus 12:44, 48).

QUESTION #3
Was circumcision a prerequisite for the original paschal sacrifice too?

ANSWER:
Reason dictates that circumcision, like the repudiation of idolatry, was a necessary prerequisite for the redemption from Egypt and, hence, for participation in the original sacrifice. The problem is that there does not appear to be an explicit reference to this in the Torah.

However, two later verses and one Midrash fill in this gap.

First, the verse we cited above (Joshua 5:2) instructed Joshua, "to circumcise the Israelites a second time (*sheinit*)." If this was to be the second time, when was the first? A subsequent verse answers: "All the people who came out [of Egypt] underwent circumcision" (5:5), suggesting that a similar mass circumcision had taken place prior to the Exodus.

A similar conclusion can be drawn from a prophecy of Ezekiel concerning Jerusalem. Describing Israel, metaphorically, as a newborn infant abandoned in the field by its parents (as Israelite parents,

---

5. On the verse: "The entire land of Egypt was starving; the people cried out to Pharaoh for bread; Pharaoh told them to go to Joseph and to do whatever he asked of them" (Genesis 41:55), Rashi (citing *Bereishit Rabbah*) commented: "Joseph had told them to be circumcised," an order they were reluctant to obey.

according to an Aggadah, did with their male offspring in Egypt), God said:

> I passed by and saw you wallowing in your own blood, and I said to you, in your blood, "live!" I said to you, in your blood, "live!" (Ezekiel 16: 6).

To what blood does this refer? A Midrash replies:

> Why did God see fit to protect them by means of blood [on the doorposts]? To remind them of the blood of Abraham's circumcision. Israel was rescued from Egypt by virtue of two types of blood: the blood of the Passover sacrifice and the blood of circumcision (*Shemot Rabbah* 17:3).[6]

Conclusion

The Exodus from Egypt figures very prominently throughout the Torah. Many *mitzvot* are linked to the Passover sacrifice demonstrating its centrality to Jewish law and lore. We have endeavored to demonstrate just how central the original Passover sacrifice (known to the Talmud as *Pesach Mitzrayim*) was to the experience of freedom and deliverance, and why its annual reenactment remains such an indispensable feature of Jewish life.

---

6. A trace of this midrashic tradition can still be found in those versions of the Haggadah following the custom of the *Ari*, that include the verse from Ezekiel 16:6 in a midrashic homily on Deuteronomy 26:5 that concludes with, "And I told you, while you bled, 'Live!' and I told you, while you bled, 'Live!'"

"Don't Sit Under the Apple Tree..."
Charoset and *Etrogim*

Preface
Our introduction to *charoset* comes via the Mishnah:

> One may not put flour into the *charoset* or into mustard, and if one did so – it must be eaten immediately (Mishnah, *Pesachim* 2:8).

According to the Mishnah commentator R. Obadiah of Bertinoro: "*Charoset* is something containing vinegar and water into which meat was dipped." And on its appearance in a later Mishnah (10:3), he added: "*Charoset* is only medicinal, to counter the acrid horseradish, which is as difficult for the body as venom."

What Are its Ingredients?
The earliest description of *charoset*'s ingredients, however, comes only from the ninth-century collection of liturgical laws and customs known as *Siddur Rav Amram Gaon*. It declares: "He should be served *charoset*... which we make out of dates."

A geonic responsum of that same century provides additional details for what appears to be a recipe for quantity cooking:

> A reminder how we make *charoset* on Pesach: To one third *hin* of strong vinegar we add fruit: 2 liters of white chestnuts – cooked before grinding, 2 liters of almonds – not shelled,

30 small dates (or 10 large ones), 800 nuts, 50 medium apples or 30 large ones.

If one cuts down on the chestnuts and almonds and adds more nuts, it will be better and nicer. Spices: ½ ounce each of yeniver, sanbal (*nard*) called aspic, canilla, askint, and pepper.... Each ingredient should be ground fine individually along with the apples as appropriate, and then ground fine again all together along with the vinegar and spices.[1]

Even Maimonides got in on the culinary act, advising in the *Mishneh Torah*:

Charoset is a rabbinic ordinance recalling the plaster [mud] they used in Egypt. How is it made? We take dates or dried figs or raisins or the like and stomp them, add vinegar and spices to resemble clay and straw, and it is served at the dinner table on Passover. (*Hilkhot Chameitz u-Matzah* 7:11)

Ashkenazi Charoset

Not surprisingly, *charoset* appeared somewhat differently in northern Europe. The earliest such source we have is from Rabbi Eliezer ben Nathan (Ra'avan; Germany 1090–1170), who prescribed: "*Charoset* is made of fruits such as apples (*tapuchim*) and nuts; spices [such as] cinnamon etc., and vegetables, such as meerettiche[2] and lettuce."

Tosafot noted, in general, that:

In geonic responsa, it is explained that *charoset* is made of fruits to which Israel is compared in the Song of Songs [such as] apples, pomegranates, figs, dates, nuts... and almonds

---

1. *Teshuvot ha-Geonim Emanuel* #40.
2. Meerettich, from Latin, meer (sea) + rettiche (radish) is a radish that grows by the sea. Apparently meer was later mistaken as mare, "horse," so sea-radish became horseradish. Cf. Arthur Schafer: "A History of Horseradish as the Bitter Herb of Passover," *Gesher* 8 (1981), 223 n. 26.

(*shekeidim*) symbolizing God's diligence (*shakad*) regarding the end of days (*Pesachim* 116a).

Raviyah (12th century) expressed a particular reservation:

> Some do not permit the use of figs in *charoset*, saying that when they are pressed into a cake, they sprinkle water on them for the flour to stick to them so they will not stick to each other. Others say that they do not sprinkle water on them and that [in any event] fruit juice does not cause *chameitz*. But whosoever refrains should continue to do so. (*Pesachim* #484)

In Provence, perhaps due to its bi-cultural Spanish-French tradition, the 13–14th century *Kol Bo* states (#50): "It is customary to put in apples…dates…nuts…and grapes…," citing in each case a biblical verse that makes reference to that ingredient.

Maharil, our fifteenth-century "go to" source for Ashkenazi customs, added a now familiar symbolic explanation, along with the ingredients themselves:

> *Charoset* recalls the clay, and atop it are cassia, cinnamon, and other spices, sliced lengthwise to recall the straw. Maharil said that some require the addition of pomegranates to dull [the maror?] (*Minhagim: Haggadah*).

But in a responsum (#25), he cautioned:

> [The Maharil ruled] that one should be wary of those small grapes called raisins because they get mixed together with dried figs in the same baskets, and we prohibit the use of dried figs because some spread flour on them.

Other Ethnic Recipes

R. Obadiah of Bertinoro described what *charoset* must have been like in Renaissance Italy:

> *Charoset* is made of figs, hazelnuts, peanuts, almonds and several types of fruit including apples. Everything is ground in a

mortar, mixed with vinegar, and topped with spices such as cassia and cinnamon [arranged] like thin threads to recall the straw. It must also be thick, recalling the clay (*Pesachim* 10:3).

In Austria, at a comparable period in time, R. Yosef b. Moshe (1423–1490) noted:

> It has been taught that it is a mitzvah to put pomegranates in *charoset* along with other fruits mentioned in the Song of Songs. It is unknown, however, why one would put pears in *charoset*, but in any event a custom should not be changed. I recall hearing from my father that putting pears in *charoset* along with apples and nuts gives it the color of red clay. It stands to reason that it must be thick like plaster, but I have seen no source that also requires the color of clay. (*Leket Yosher* I, 83, #5)

The custom of Safed is reflected in the work of R. Yosef Karo (1488–1575):

> The *Mordekhai* (*Pesach* #284) wrote in the name of the *Rokeach* that we put cassia, cinnamon, and ginger into the *charoset*, because they cannot be ground well without leaving tough strands that recall the straw that was mixed with the clay. (*Beit Yosef Orach Chayim* 473:5)

The Chida, R. Chayyim Yosef David Azulai (Israel and Italy, 1724–1806), told of some whose quest for authenticity in charoset went too far:

> There are those who put some clay or brick dust [into *charoset*] to recall the clay... I was frightened to see such nonsense. On Purim, do they draw blood to recall the fatal edict? One is obliged [on Passover] to transform sorrow into joy and evil into goodness. (*Birkei Yosef* 473:12)[3]

---

3. The Chida attributed this strange practice to a misprint in the text of the

Elsewhere, the peripatetic Chida noted yet another variation on the *charoset* theme:

> In Salonica, the custom is to make *charoset* mainly out of chestnuts (*'armonim*), which is perplexing because Israel was not compared to chestnuts... although I found a precedent for it in the commentary of R. Manoah to Maimonides (Op. cit., 473:13).

Charoset in Galicia

Perhaps the most innovative approach to *charoset*, however, was that of R. Hanokh Teitelbaum (Sassov/Galicia; 1884–1943), author of the responsa *Yad Chanokh*. Here (#8), he replied to a correspondent who questioned the rabbi's insistence that one ingredient of *charoset* must be *etrog*.

> I received your letter stating that you have heard it said in my name that one should put *etrog* into *charoset*. You are suspicious because you have never heard of such a thing and because the Jewish custom is to use apples, nuts, and other fruits whose mnemonic is *charoset 'eitz* and *charoset 'even*.[4]
>
> You ask for my reasoning, so here it is. *Charoset* should be made from fruits to which the Jewish people have been compared, and according to R. Akiva (BT *Shabbat* 88a), they are compared to a *tapuach* (Songs 2:3), whose tree bears blossoms before its leaves. Tosafot (ad. loc.), however, raised the question that apple trees are really no different from other fruit-bearing trees and do not bear blossoms before leaves. Therefore, R.

---

commentaries of Rashbam and Rashi to *Pesachim* 116a that substituted *cheres* (a pottery shard used to grind the ingredients) for *charoset*. For an inventive use of an actual brick in lieu of *charoset*, see the postscript to this chapter.

4. A pun on Exodus 31:5: *charoshet 'even* (cut stones) and *charoshet 'eitz* (carved wood), *charoset 'eitz* would imply fruit, like apples, while *charoset 'even* suggests something harder, like nuts.

Tam explained that the *tapuach* refers to the *etrog*, whose fruit does precede its blossoms. That is why we put *etrog* into the *charoset*.

In the continuation, he even denied the nigh universal assumption that apples are an indispensable ingredient of *charoset*:

> If the principle is to make *charoset* out of fruits to which the Jewish people were compared, then there is a Midrash (*Vayikra Rabbah* 30) that compares them to *peri 'eitz hadar*.... It appears to me that the universal custom of putting a fruit called "apple" in *charoset* is not because Israel is compared to apples but for another reason... to recall that they used to deliver their children in Egypt beneath apple trees so the Egyptians would not notice them, to wit: "I have awakened you beneath the *tapuach*".... (Song 8:5)

R. Tam, too, admitted that the reference is not to an *etrog* tree but to the apple tree (appelbaum) because it is pleasant to lie beneath it during a heat-spell and to take shelter in its branches that spread out to all sides and provide concealment: "This is not the case with an *etrog* tree, so the verse 'beneath the *tapuach*' clearly refers to an apple tree."

How could one ensure the availability of *etrogim* in the springtime? R. Teitlbaum was ready for that, too:

> In that case, one might save his *etrog* from Sukkot until Passover in order to compound its use for a mitzvah – just as it is said of the Maharil that he saved the *hosha'not* from Sukkot to fuel the fire to burn *chameitz*.[5]

---

5. The custom of placing the *'aravot* atop the *'aron ha-kodesh*, in a not atypical fashion, has devolved in many synagogues into throwing the *lulav* atop the *'aron* complete with *'aravot* and *hadassim*. Nowadays, a recognizable use for an *etrog* after the holiday is in making jelly. Some people leave them in a closet because they give off a pleasant aroma until they dry up.

Postscript: *Charoset* in the Civil War

The Chida, as noted above, was aghast at those who put clay or brick dust into *charoset*. Little did he imagine that something quite similar would find its way onto the battlefields of the American Civil War. In 1862, the following account of a *seder* celebrated by Union soldiers in Fayette, West Virginia, was reported by J.A. Joel of the 23rd Ohio Volunteer Regiment. A fellow soldier, returning from home leave, had supplied his comrades in arms with *matzot* and *haggadot*. The rest was ad hoc.

> We... sen[t] parties to forage in the country [for Passover food] while a party stayed to build a log hut for the services.... We obtained two kegs of cider, a lamb, several chickens and some eggs. Horseradish or parsley we could not obtain, but in lieu we found a weed whose bitterness, I apprehend, exceeded anything our forefathers 'enjoyed.'... We had the lamb, but did not know what part was to represent it at the table; but Yankee ingenuity prevailed, and it was decided to cook the whole and put it on the table, then we could dine off it, and be sure we got the right part.
>
> The necessaries for the choroutzes (!) we could not obtain, so we got a brick which, rather hard to digest, reminded us, by looking at it, for what purpose it was intended.[6]

---

6. *The Jewish Messenger*, March 30, 1866.

Shir Ha-Shirim Inside and Out
The Perspective of Rav Kook

Preface

Whenever *Shir ha-Shirim* is studied, someone is bound to ask: Am I permitted to examine the literal side of this text; i.e., that which appears to be a romantic poem of love between one man and one woman, or may I only consider it allegorically; i.e., as symbolizing the relationship between God and the Jewish nation?

Rav Kook answered that it is permissible to examine the literal side of the text providing one's examination takes place within the proper milieu and takes the proper Torah perspective.[1] Our aim in this chapter is to explore two dimensions of this bold statement: the aesthetic and the allegorical. We shall proceed primarily by way of Rav Kook's own essay on the subject, with explanatory references to the positions of Maimonides and the Zohar. We shall also consider the text of Rashi's singular and exceptional introduction to *Shir ha-Shirim*, and will attempt to clarify his view, and that of Ibn Ezra, on the relationship between the literal sense of a text and its metaphorical or allegorical treatment.

Aesthetics and Allegory

The first word we have to say about aesthetics and allegory concerns poetry. In the opening paragraph of his essay, Rav Kook stipulated

---

1. Our source is Rav Kook's commentary on *Shir ha-Shirim*, which is published in volume 2 of his *siddur*, *'Olat Re'iyah* (Jerusalem: Mosad Harav Kook).

that "as long as one sketch, which is revealed in the profundity of the sensitive rational soul, remains absent and unfulfilled, there is an obligation upon the artistic impulse (*'avodat ha'omanut*) to bring it to fruition." By a sketch, he meant a creative idea that has only begun to take shape, and his point is that the role and responsibility of aesthetics is to bring that sketch of an idea to its tangible realization in literature, art, or sculpture.

Since poetic language is, conventionally, the foremost dimension of literature that brings spiritual concepts to fruition, it would serve us well to see what Rav Kook wrote of his own inclination towards the poetic. In *Arpelei Tohar*, he explained why he chose to write in a very lyrical Hebrew style:

> My thoughts are as wide as the ocean and I cannot express them in prose. Against my best interests, I must become a poet, but only in free verse. I cannot be bound and shackled by meter and rhyme. I am escaping from simple prose because it is too cumbersome, because it is too constricting. I cannot place upon myself additional restrictions that might be greater and even more profound than the constraints of prose that I am escaping.

What were Rav Kook's "best interests," which he feared would not be served by traditional poetry? One assumes he meant clarity and comprehension. He appreciated that the freedom of expression that poetry lent to his spirituality was countered by the risk he was running of either being dismissed as esoteric, or – what would be even worse – misunderstood. Yet he considered this risk to be worthwhile.

Indeed, we may pause here to consider whether King Solomon weighed similar alternatives before committing *Shir ha-Shirim* to posterity. On the one hand, his use of poetic imagery manifestly extended his ability to describe the beauty, commitment, and passion of his subjects. On the other hand, however, that same poetry throws his outer focus (the shepherdess, *ro'ah*, and her beloved, *dod*) into such sharp relief that it becomes its own worst enemy, obscuring the inner dimension (God and the Jewish nation), which is its only biblical *raison d'être*.

Now that we have introduced the notion of an "outer" and an "inner" focus (or dimension) to *Shir ha-Shirim*, let us point out that rabbinic and medieval Jewish thought operated on this multi-dimensional premise, which, interestingly enough, was shared by rationalists and mystics alike. To demonstrate this point, we have chosen two sources: the *Moreh Nevukhim* of the arch-rationalist Maimonides, and the Zohar, the crucible of the mystical Kabbalah. We shall cite a representative passage from each, briefly describe their similarities and differences, and apply them to Rav Kook's assessment of *Shir ha-Shirim*.

We shall further suggest that Rav Kook's conclusion regarding the mutual coexistence in *Shir ha-Shirim* of romantic love (*'ahavah*) and the spiritual love of God (*'ahavah ha-kedoshah*) is implicit in Rashi's introduction to the book, and explicit in Abraham Ibn Ezra's methodological approach to it.

Tanakh Inside and Out

The proposition that individual words and whole verses of Tanakh have multiple meanings is so unmistakable in the Talmud and the Midrash as to require no repetition here. Rather, our concern is with the question of how different levels of meaning, visible to different people, exist simultaneously in the very same texts.[2]

Maimonides

In his introduction to the *Guide for the Perplexed*, Maimonides explained his choice of the title as follows:

> This treatise also has a second purpose: namely, the explanation of very obscure parables occurring in the books of the prophets,

---

2. Cf. Frank E. Talmage: "Apples of Gold; The Inner Meaning of Sacred Texts in Medieval Judaism," in *Apples of Gold in Settings of Silver* (Toronto, 1999), 108 ff.

but not explicitly identified there as such. Hence an ignorant or heedless individual might think that they possess only an external sense, but no internal one. However, even when one who truly possesses knowledge considers these parables and interprets them according to their external meaning, he, too, is overtaken by great perplexity. But if we explain these parables to him or if we draw his attention to their being parables, he will take the right road and be delivered from this perplexity. That is why I have called this treatise the *Guide for the Perplexed*.

Maimonides, then, assumed that:

1. The Bible, which speaks in a human idiom (*bi-l'shon b'nei 'adam*), is intended to instruct all people, ignorant as well as learned.
2. It speaks on two levels, one outer (exoteric) and the other inner (esoteric).
3. Biblical texts must be intelligible on both levels – the exoteric to the uninitiated and the esoteric to the enlightened.

Indeed, the philosopher Leo Strauss, in *Persecution and the Art of Writing*, argued that the *Guide*, like the biblical parables it sought to explain, likewise operates on two levels, with Maimonides simultaneously addressing a lay audience and a philosophically enlightened audience, albeit on different levels.

Zohar

The Zohar also accepts this two-dimensional premise, which it calls "open" and "sealed," and seeks to establish the transcendent significance of even the Torah's most mundane passages:

> Come and see: There are garments that everyone sees, and when fools see a man in a garment that seems beautiful to them, they do not look more closely. But more important than the body is the soul.... Fools see only the garment which is the narrative part of the Torah; they know no more and fail to

see what is under the garment. Those who know more see not only the garment but also the body that is under the garment. But the truly wise ... look only upon the soul which is the true foundation of the entire Torah.

Rashi and Ibn Ezra on *Shir HaShirim*

A. RASHI

Rav Kook's point about the compatibility of romantic love and spiritual love – which he portrayed as two mutual dimensions of *Shir ha-Shirim* – is essentialy Rashi's viewpoint as well.

Rashi did not customarily compose introductions to his commentaries, so his introdiuction to *Shir ha-Shirim* is even more singular and significant.

> "God speaks but once, yet I hear two messages" (Psalms 62:12). A single verse may have several meanings, but, in final analysis, no verse may be purged of its literal sense. And even though the prophets were wont to speak figuratively (*be-dugma'*), one must settle the figure within its context as per the sequential arrangement of the scriptural texts.[3]

Two observations are in order, one about the Rashi text and one about the translation. First of all, the *Mikra'ot Gedolot*'s reading of *peshuto u-masha'o* is clearly unreliable. Whether it should remain *peshuto*, as in the talmudic idiom, or *mashma'o* – which is the reading of many reliable manuscripts and printed editions[4] – is irrelevant to the English translation, which is "literal" in either case, since even the word *peshuto* is defined by the Amora Rabba (*Yevamot* 24a) as *mamash*, "literal."

---

3. See Moshe Sokolow, *Tanakh, an Owner's Manual: Authorship, Canonization, Masoretic Text, Exegesis, Modern Scholaryship and Pedagogy* (Urim, 2015), 95–96: "Literary Sensitivity."
4. We follow the critical edition published by Judah Rosenthal in *The Samuel K. Mirsky Jubilee Volume* (NY, 1958).

We see here that while Rashi was certainly aware of the allegorical nature of *Shir ha-Shirim*, he made that figurative meaning contingent upon its literal sense and upon its context. Without understanding the pastoral context of the book and without first delving into its "exoteric" meaning, we cannot adequately comprehend its figurative function. Just as someone who takes a verse out of its sequential context can make it say something sage and significant that it promptly ceases to mean once it has been restored to its proper place, so we must not take *Shir ha-Shirim* out of its traditional-cultural context and make it say something literal that it ceases to mean once it is returned to the allegorical context in which Rabbi Akiva saw it (see below).

B. IBN EZRA

Ibn Ezra, the paradigm of rational anti-mystical exegesis, stipulated in his own introduction:

> God forbid that *Shir ha-Shirim* should be regarded as an ordinary love poem, rather than figuratively.

He, too, was aware of the contingent relationship between a figure of speech and its literal sense, hence he divided his own commentary into three parts:

1. the literal, dictionary definition of each word;
2. understood according to its literal sense; and
3. understood as an allegory.

Rav Kook

Rav Kook, as an heir to both spiritual traditions, also presumed the multi-dimensional nature of Tanakh, and endeavored – in his characteristic fashion – to demonstrate their mutual coexistence. He, too, was aware of the penchant of the uninformed to be satisfied with the superficial, and he, too, was sympathetic to the perplexity of even the enlightened when dealing with difficult parables. Hence, his stern admonition (delivered in paragraph I C, below) against revealing thoughts that are best kept concealed, and his unsparing criticism (II-C, IV-A) of the "boor about love" and the "bleary-eyed midgets" who insist on bringing the Torah down to their own mundane level, rather than striving to elevate themselves to its lofty heights.

I. A Rabbi Akiva said: God forbid! No Jew ever denied that *Shir ha-Shirim* defiles the hands. Indeed, the entire world is not as worthwhile as the day on which *Shir ha-Shirim* was composed. For all Scriptures are holy, and *Shir ha-Shirim* is the Holy of Holies (Mishnah, *Yadayim* 3:5).[5]

   B Literature, art and sculpture are capable of putting into practice all the spiritual concepts which are ingrained in the depths of the human soul, and as long as even one sketch which is revealed in the profundity of the sensitive rational soul remains absent and unfulfilled, there is an obligation upon the creative impulse to bring it to fruition.

   C It is self-understood that only those treasures whose development freshens the air of reality are worthy of being developed just as the world was filled with aromatic spices from every word uttered by God [at Sinai]. Those hidden things, however, which should be removed and buried, are best left for the spade to bury and conceal, and woe unto him who uses that spade to uncover them and their foul stench.

II A The agitation caused to the soul by the feelings of natural love – which play a large role in reality, morality, and life – deserves to be explained by literature in all of the many ways in which it

---

5. Explaining "defiling the hands" as a euphemism for scriptural canonization, the Talmud stated: "Why did [the Sages] enact that a scroll defiles [one's hands]? Rav Mesharshiya said: Originally, people would store *terumah* food alongside Torah scrolls, saying, "this is holy and that is holy." When they saw that this caused a loss [according to Rashi, mice, attracted by the grain, would eat the scrolls], the Sages enacted the defilement" (*Shabbat* 13b). Cf. Sokolow: *TANAKH, op. cit.*, 50 ff.

brings the concealed to light, but only if it exercises the utmost caution lest it incline towards the ugly intoxication which such feelings arouse and which transform them from their natural purity to an impurity of contemptuous loathing. Only holy men deserve to become holy poets.

B If it is considered a general deficiency in literature, however, when these innermost feelings that love conventionally impresses upon the depths of the soul are absent, then how much more so is it a deficiency if those same lofty and sublime tremors (because this is how they always act and will always act upon all the best men and on the Jewish collective (*Keneset Yisrael*) in particular), which derive from the wellspring of love of the Master of all things, the source of light and of grace; if these lovely feelings are not recorded in the Book and their absence is noted? Can the depths of the wellspring of this emotion of love be measured? Can it be contained by great oceans or sustained by lofty heights?

C It is this very deficiency which has been filled for us in the love poem, that very poem which is the Holy of Holies, namely the (choicest) song of Solomon's songs! Indeed, someone who is a boor about love will not sense what the poets of love are trying to say in their personal poems, and if he had the opportunity to degrade their yearnings to the level of his own vulgar feelings he would gladly and delightedly do so. (Only one who is emotionally opaque would necessarily do so because he has never attempted to aspire to [the poem's] sanctified sublimity and has never felt the intense pleasure of the light of the Source of the Universe.) An ignorant fool such as he cannot grasp the idea that the many personal yearnings expressed in *Shir ha-Shirim* are traces of the treasure hidden in the hearts of the entire nation which God elected to bear His name and recognition, because this fool cannot be sensitive to the absence of these feelings which he has never known himself.

III A Someone whom God has not deprived of wisdom, however, will recognize and realize that it is entirely impossible in the context of the holy Scriptures of the holy nation whose history is filled with traces of spiritual love for its fortress and refuge – in its period of grandeur by means of sublime grace and dignity, and in its period of poverty and persecution by means of torrents of blood and waves of pain and distress all of which aroused this love, reinforced it, and brought it to tangible actualization – it is entirely impossible for such yearnings not to leave their traces in the Book, the national treasury wherein all its sacred expressions are stored.

B Nevertheless, he [i.e., Rabbi Akiva] who could reply, while they tore at his flesh with iron combs, "All my life I despaired over the verse, '[And you shall love the Lord your God with all your heart and] with all your soul...' when will I have the opportunity to fulfill it?," and who could prolong the word "[the Lord is] One" until death overcame him; only he could have said that the entire world was not as worthwhile as the day on which *Shir ha-Shirim* was given to Israel, for if all Scripture is holy, then *Shir ha-Shirim* is the Holy of Holies.

C Even as a drop of water to the sea, even as a single spark to a blazing flame, even as a single letter to a voluminous book, so did this man of sublime spirit know the value of even private love in its purity, combining pure natural love, enlightened national love, and the sacred and divine love into a resplendent edifice like the many-turreted Tower of David.

IV A How insignificant are those bleary-eyed midgets who crawl about the lowest level of stones of a fortified tower and delineate its height – which is skyscraping – only so far as their puny hands and shortsighted vision can reach. If they were told that from the top of that tower they could gaze upon a splendid and brilliant star, they would immediately decide that the superb star must really be insignificant. People such as these, who cannot see in Rabbi Akiva more than the tender-hearted shepherd who loved the beautiful daughter of Kalba Savua, likewise cannot recognize any source for the essence of that wonderful resolution comparing the value of *Shir ha-Shirim* in Scripture to that of the Holy of Holies, other than the source of commonplace love which, alone, they recognize in Rabbi Akiva who loved the daughter of Kalba Savua....

B The pure of heart, however, see Rabbi Akiva in his grandeur: the Rabbi Akiva who could smile while seeing a fox emerge from the site of the Holy of Holies because his lofty spirit could draw nigh the distant future [of redemption]; the Rabbi Akiva who rejoiced at the tumultuous sounds of Rome because the divine love emanating from the depths of his spacious heart indicated to him – as though in a completely animated picture – that Rome and its idols would disappear entirely while the light of Zion would shine eternally.

C His enraptured delight with the vision of the future so filled his pure heart that it left no room for dwelling upon the frightful present which he saw only as a slight cloud passing before a brilliant sun. Only in the name of the man who died with "One" on his lips is it fitting to quote: "If all Scriptures are holy, *Shir ha-Shirim* is the Holy of Holies."[6]

---

6. On Rabbi Akiva as a role model for Jewish character education, see my review of Barrry W. Holz: *Rabbi Akiva, Sage of the Talmud* (New Haven: Yale, 2017) in *Journal of Jewish Studies* 83:4 (2017), 393–395.

Flowering Trees . . . Flourishing Redemption
The Prayer for the Welfare of the State of Israel

Preface
Shortly after the State of Israel was established in 1948, Ashkenazi Chief Rabbi Isaac Herzog, with the assistance of Sephardi Chief Rabbi Ben-Zion Meir Chai Uziel, composed a "Prayer for the Welfare of the State" (*Tefillah li-Sh'lom ha-Medinah*), which was edited on their behalf by S.Y. Agnon. (Claims that Agnon, winner of the 1966 Nobel Prize in literature, was the actual author, may be refuted – not in the least part – by the fact that Agnon, neither reticent nor unassertive by nature, never laid claim to it himself.)

While many Jewish communities never adopted it at all and others confined its recitation to Israel's Independence Day, even those who were in overall ideological agreement with the newfound state and recited it regularly found elements of the prayer problematic.

Reishit Tzemichat Ge'ulateinu
Indeed, the most controversial phrase appears prominently in its opening sentence:

> Our Father in Heaven, Rock of Israel and its Redeemer, bless the State of Israel, the first flowering of our redemption (*reishit tzemichat ge'ulateinu*).

Most of the attempts to emend (or corrupt) the prayer consist of either the complete elimination of the phrase "the first flowering of our redemption," or the interpolation before it of the verb *tehei*, "let it be," rejecting the implication that the redemption had already begun and, thereby, postponing it to the eschatological future.

I would like to make the argument that it is precisely the discord between the anticipation of redemption and its ostensible delay that validates the original wording.

Birkhat Hallanot

To do so, we need to call attention to a seemingly unrelated ritual: the springtime blessing over fruit trees in bloom. The Talmud instructs:

> One who goes about during Nisan and sees [fruit] trees in bloom should say: "Blessed [is He] who spared nothing in His world, and created therein goodly creatures and goodly trees for people to enjoy themselves thereby." (*Berakhot* 43b)

Recognizing God as the author of creation is to acknowledge Him as the fount of aesthetics as well. Yet more than just aesthetics impels the performance of this ritual. It is bound up with the historical springtime redemption from Egypt, on the one hand, and with the ultimate redemption, on the other.

The Torah states: "Today you are leaving [Egypt], in the season of the ripening barley (*chodesh he'aviv*)" (Exodus 13:4), confirming that the original Exodus occurred simultaneously with the inception of the barley harvest – an event that we mark by commencing the counting of the *'omer* on the second night of Passover. Indeed, the reason that the Jewish calendar accommodates both the 354-day lunar year and the 365-day solar year (through the intermittent addition of a thirteenth month) is to ensure that Passover – dated 15 Nisan – is perpetually celebrated early in the spring.[1]

---

1. See "Who Sanctified the 4th... of December?" above.

Trees and Redemption

The Talmud recognizes the springtime flowering of fruit trees as the surest sign of the imminent redemption of the Jewish people. Citing the verse "You, the mountains of Israel, give forth your branches and bear fruit for my people of Israel for their return is near" (Ezekiel 36:8), it stipulates, "There is no end [of time] more explicit than that" (*Sanhedrin* 98a). Indeed, the recurring cycle of bloom and decline that characterizes trees in general is a natural paradigm for the wax and wane of individual as well as national fortunes (cf. Psalms 1:3, 92:13, inter alia.).

A crucial provision of the blessing over a flowering tree, however, is that it can be recited only over the appearance of its blossoms:

> If one postpones the blessing until after the tree has borne fruit, he shall no longer recite it. (*Shulchan 'Arukh Orach Chayyim* 226:1)

The "Prayer for the Welfare of the State of Israel" takes the analogy between trees and redemption to its logical conclusion: Just as the blessing over fruit bearing trees is made over the blossoms – representing the promise of fruition – rather than over the fruit itself, so should the prayer for the welfare of the State of Israel be recited over the "first flourishing of our redemption," rather than over its complete fulfillment.

Measuring Redemption and "Hope"

Our Sages taught us that redemption must be recognized as a measured process and not as an instantaneous achievement:

> "Who is she that shines like the dawn?" (Song of Songs 6:10). R. Hiyya and R. Shimon bar Halafta were walking through the Arbel valley at the glimmering [of dawn] and they saw the light of the morning star breaking through. Said R. Hiyya the elder to R. Shimon bar Halafta: "So will the redemption of

Israel peek out, to wit: 'As I sit in darkness, the Lord will be my light' (Micah 7:8). At first, it approaches gradually; afterwards it sparkles; then it waxes, ever refreshing, as it advances." (*Shir haShirim Rabbah* 6)

Moreover, sometimes the faint glimmer of redemption can be perceived only when it is viewed against a "background" of suffering and oppression that preceded it. The State of Israel was founded in the season of arboreal rebirth and at an historical junction of national death (the Holocaust) and resurgence.

An Ideological Justification

From his perspective as a Holocaust survivor and veteran of the War of Independence, Rav Yehudah Amital, z"l, was singularly attuned to the dissonance between the promise of redemption that he and others identified in the Zionist enterprise and the setbacks it experienced on the way of its unfolding – of which the Holocaust was but one. In an address he delivered on Israel Independence Day 1993, he pointed to the paradox:

> Students of the Vilna Gaon spoke of the "beginning of the redemption," R. Eliyahu Guttmacher of Graidetz spoke of the "beginning of the redemption," and Rav Kook also spoke of the "beginning of the redemption." Yet after all these came the Holocaust.[2]

And on another occasion, he elaborated:

> The combination of salvation and sorrow in this world of ours, in which God's name and God's throne are not complete, is a too-common combination. Salvation and sorrow usually co-exist. It is the way of the world that every great salvation in

---

2. Elyashiv Reichner, *By Faith Alone: The story of Rabbi Yehuda Amital* (Jerusalem: Maggid, 2011), 202–203.

battle comes with sorrow, and usually at the price of sorrow. But sometimes the grief is so great, so all-encompassing, so deep, and so galling, that a man's heart is too narrow to include both feelings – the feeling of salvation alongside the feeling of sorrow. Then it is as though the salvation is dwarfed, until it even becomes grief.[3]

His juxtaposition of "salvation and sorrow" is not an innovation of the twentieth century; R. Shelomo Ephraim Luntschitz (1550–1619) struck the identical pose in his Torah commentary, *Keli Yakar*. The exile, he explained, is comparable to death, and redemption from exile is the renewal of life because it enables Israel to exist both nationally and religiously. He drew our attention to one verse in particular:

> See now that it is truly I and there is no deity with Me. I take life and grant it; I smite and heal; there is no escape from My might. (Deut. 32:39)

He explained that the repetition of the word "I," whose duplication is reminiscent of "Comfort ye, comfort ye, My people" (Isa. 40:1) and "I, I am He who comforts you" (Isa. 51:12), is a reference to the twofold redemption that is to come: physical and spiritual; physical redemption from our political subjugation by the nations of the world and spiritual redemption from our capitulation to the evil inclination.

> This is the meaning of the Rabbis' assertion that we learn the principle of resurrection from this verse; that is redemption, for in exile we are like the dead. And at the time of redemption, God will make us live. He has already resurrected us from the exiles of Egypt and Babylon, but these redemptions were not eternal. "And on the third day" (Hosea 6:2), which is a reference to the third redemption, he will make us live for all eternity before him. (*Keli Yakar*, Deut. 32:39)

---

3. *By Faith Alone*, 99.

Our Hope

Poignantly, this very concurrence of national tragedy and promise was anticipated in the nineteenth century by an inspired Zionist poet, Naftali Herz Imber (1856–1909), who enshrined it in his immortal ode, Tikvateinu ("Our Hope," 1886), later transformed into Ha-Tikvah ("The Hope"), first the Zionist and then the Israeli national anthem.

Often overlooked is that the poem's title draws upon Ezekiel's famous prophetic vision in which he saw a valley full of dry bones. God promised to connect them to one another, cover them with flesh and skin, and inspire them to return to life. He then explained to the prophet what the bones and their resurrection represent:

> [God] said to me: "Son of Man, these bones are the entire House of Israel. They are saying: Our bones have dried, our hope is lost (*'avedah tikvateinu*), and our fate is decreed." Therefore, prophesy to them saying: "Thus says the Lord, God. Behold I shall open your graves, my people, remove you from them, and bring you to the Land of Israel." (37:11–12)

Like Ezekiel, Imber foresaw the resurrection of the Jewish nation and, by reversing "our hope is lost" into "our hope is not yet lost" (*'od lo avedah tikvateinu*), gave lyrical expression to its renaissance and efflorescence; an affirmation of hope in the face of tragedy, of life seized from the jaws of death.

What could be more worthy of a blessing than the first flourishing of that long-anticipated redemption?

Bakeish Shalom VeRodefeihu
The "Pursuit" of Peace

Preface

For close to two millennia, i.e., since the destruction of the Second Temple, questions of determining war and peace were only theoretical for Jews. Among all post-talmudic authorities, Maimonides alone dealt with them as matters of legal principle.[1] Only with the establishment of the State of Israel did they resume their earlier normative character – and since then, mostly on the war side of the ledger. In September of 1993, however, as it appeared that Israel and the Palestinians were on the verge of making peace, the discussion of peace resumed its place on the Jewish agenda, and has recurred, sporadically, on any number of subsequent occasions. Let us look at what classic

---

1. Cf. Aviezer Ravitzky: "Peace," in Arthur A. Cohen and Paul Mendes-Flohr (eds.): *Contemporary Jewish Religious Thought* (NY, 1987), 691:

> Throughout Jewish history, neither war nor peace really stood as concrete options for the Jewish people. The Jew, lacking political sovereignty, had no status in the international debate, and the question of war or peace in the here and now did not press him for an immediate response or decision. Only the wars of the Gentiles belonged to concrete historical reality, and that reality was the Jew's involuntary lot.
>
> On the other hand, the ancient wars of Israel were a matter more for theology than for politics. They took place in Scripture, either in the distant past or, at the approach of the messianic age, in the distant future.

Jewish sources have to say about the nature of peace, and what they prescribe for obtaining it.

Option or Obligation

On the verses: "Whoever desires life and is eager for years of goodness... Avoid evil, do good, seek peace, and pursue it" (Psalms 34:13–15), a Midrash comments:

> Great is peace. All other *mitzvot* are prefaced by: "If you see...," "If you meet...," "If it occurs..." [In other words,] if a mitzvah presents itself, you are required to perform it; otherwise, you are not obligated. Here, however, it says: "Seek peace and pursue it"; seek it wherever you may be and pursue it wherever it may be. (*Leviticus Rabbah* 9:9)

Messianic Peace

Despite a divine mandate to rule over Gentile nations by force, if necessary, the Messiah, according to a Midrash, will first try to address them peacefully. Yet another Midrash describes peace as the harbinger of Israel's redemption and Jerusalem's consolation. And a normative halakhic statement in the Mishnah condemns weapons of war as "contemptible."

> "I am peace and so shall I speak" (Ps. 120:7) What is meant by "I am peace"? God said to the Messiah: "Rule them with an iron staff" (Ps. 2:9). Said he: Master of the Universe, No! I shall begin, rather, by addressing the nations peacefully. (*Midrash Tehillim* 120)
>
> Great is peace, since God will announce Israel's redemption only in peace (*Devarim Rabbah* 5:15).
>
> Peace is beloved [*chaviv*], since God will console Jerusalem only in peace (*Devarim Rabbah* 5:14).
>
> It is prohibited for a man to go out [into the public domain on Shabbat] with a sword, bow, shield, dagger, or spear. Rabbi

Eliezer says they are ornaments [and are permissible]. But the Sages say they are contemptible [*genai*], as it is written: "They shall beat their swords into plowshares..." (Isaiah 2:4). (Mishnah, *Shabbat* 6:4)²

Maimonides on Peace

Maimonides depicted peace as the true natural state of man, a state that was interrupted by "primeval sin" and awaits redemption from the abyss of violence into which mankind has been plunged due to impulse and emotionalism.³

> Just as a blind man who cannot see, stumbles, injures himself, and causes harm to others... Groups of people, due to their stupidity, grievously harm themselves and others... Through knowledge of truth, enmity and strife are averted and people will no longer harm each other. The reason for the disappearance of hatreds, hostility and struggles, will be people's awareness, at that time, of the Divine truth. (*Guide for the Perplexed* 3:11)

---

2. Additional significance attaches to this passage as one of only three places in the Talmud to feature the seminal phrase: *'ein mikra' yotzei miyedei peshuto* (Scripture can never be purged of its literal sense).
3. Maimonides viewed the vision of peace foretold by the prophets as a natural and necessary outgrowth of the domination of the intellect over man's destructive impulses. According to him, violence and war, people inflicting harm on one another, have their source in irrationality and ignorance. However, the apprehension of truth – "knowledge of God" – displaces man's awareness from his attachment to illusory goods and interests, and completely eliminates the irrational factors that arouse mutual conflict between individuals, groups and nations. As Ravitzky put it:

> Intellectual perfection is the guarantor of peace. This follows not upon a change in man's nature, but rather upon the fulfillment and realization of his rational self, an overcoming, as it were, of original sin, which is interpreted by Maimonides as man's fall from the world of intellect and apprehension to the world of lust, conflict, and struggle between good and evil. (693–694)

In another passage, Maimonides maintained that Israel has no "political" ambitions (for world domination, etc.), but desires peace solely in order to promote the study of Torah. This last passage is exceptionally significant because it appears in the *Mishneh Torah*, as a normative *halakhah*, rather than in one of his more populist works.

> Neither the Sages nor the Prophets desired the Messianic Age either to rule the world, oppress the Gentiles, be honored by the nations, or in order to eat, drink and be merry. Rather, [they desired it only] in order to devote themselves to Torah and its wisdom, without oppression or interruption. (*Hilkhot Melakhim* 12:4)

A Non-Maimonidean View

In contrast to Maimonides, who saw peace as the triumph of rationalism, Rabbi Abraham bar Hiyya (Spain, 1070–1136) conceived of peace as a "divine intervention" that alters human nature and stimulates universal observance of the mitzvah to "love your neighbor as yourself."

> This mitzvah will pertain to, and be fulfilled by, all the inhabitants of the world in those [Messianic] days. If all the world's inhabitants will love one another as one loves on behalf of himself, then – quite naturally – enmity, hostility, and envy will be eradicated from the world. These, indeed, are the very factors that produce war and killing in this world. (*Hegyon ha-Nefesh*, Chapter 4)

Rav Kook on Peace

Rabbi Abraham I. Kook (1865–1935) also depicted the constant state of war (particularly in the Middle East) as the consequence of sin, albeit a different one: the sin of the Golden Calf. Peace, he wote: "has been delayed" on that account; postponed, but not eliminated forever.

> Were it not for the sin of the Golden Calf, the Gentile inhabitants of Israel would have made peace with Israel. No wars would

have ensued. Instead, the inclination would have been towards peace – as in the Messianic era. But sin interfered and this has been delayed for thousands of years. (*Orot ha-Kodesh*, p. 14)

Peace Grounded in Humanity

The Torah reports that as the reunion between the patriarch Jacob and his brother Esau drew near, "Jacob was greatly afraid and distressed" (Genesis 32:8). A Midrash parses the verse as follows: "He feared greatly, lest he be killed. He was distressed, lest he kill" (*Midrash Aggadah Bereishit*, ad. loc.). In our own times, Golda Meir paraphrased this sentiment when she famously said:

> We can forgive the Arabs for killing our children. We cannot forgive them for forcing us to kill their children. We will have peace with the Arabs only when they love their children more than they hate us.[4]

In the light of Israel's ongoing struggle against terrorism, consider the poignancy of the impassioned plea for a peace grounded in humanity that was issued by a former Chief Rabbi of Great Britain:

> A medieval Jewish source movingly tells us that one hundred shofar sounds at our New Year services correspond to the one hundred groans by the mother of Sisera (Judges 5:28) when she saw her son killed in battle against the Israelites.
>
> Sisera was a brutal tyrant, wreaking terror on our people. His death was our salvation. Yet, he had a mother, and to this day we hear her cries and recall her grief over the death of her child.
>
> Even terrorists have mothers, and we must not be indifferent to their anguish. This is but one of the remarkable features

---

4. Ostensibly made at a National Press Club appearance, there is reason to question whether the statement was made at that time – or at all. See https://www.haaretz.com/golda-meir-s-gems-did-she-really-say-that-1.5371930.

of Judaism in an effort to ensure that even war does not harden us to the point of not caring for the loss and suffering of our enemies.[5]

While the mothers of some terrorist "martyrs" may exhibit pride in their children's deaths and, sometimes, even accept financial rewards for their activities, one would like to believe that in their heart of hearts they rue their extremism and would join forces with the mothers of their victims to put an end to the suffering on both sides and bring peace.

---

5. Sir Immanuel Jacobovitz: "The Morality of Warfare," *Le'eylah* 2:4 (1983).

Yeshiva Students and Military Service
The Origin of Hesder

Preface

In 1998, the Israeli Supreme Court ruled that the exemption of yeshiva students (*b'nei yeshivah*) from military service that had been in force since the founding of the State of Israel in 1948 had no basis in Israeli law, and instructed the Knesset to adopt appropriate legislation on the matter. The Tal commission (named for its chair, the former Supreme Court justice Tzvi Tal) that investigated the issue determined that drafting yeshiva students and Torah teachers could shorten compulsory military service for all Israelis by four months, reduce the age for mandatory reserve duty, and cut in half the amount of time reservists needed to be called for operational purposes.

Nevertheless, no new legislation was adopted, and since then the issue has seesawed back and forth as internal Israeli politics alternately raised and lowered the value of Hareidi parties to ruling government coalitions, which have, alternately, extended the exemption or threatened to revoke it. A recent such swing occurred in November 2015, resulting in the extension of the accommodation for Hareidim for another four years. The elimination of Hareidi parties from the newly elected (June 2021) Bennet-Lapid government has placed the issue back on the front burner of Israeli politics.

This exemption touches a most sensitive chord, particularly in anyone who values the three guiding principles of religious Zionism: the Land of Israel, the Jewish nation, and the Torah (*'eretz yisrael,* 'am yisrael, torat yisrael). Whereas some (on the "right") have their misgivings about the value of the state and others (on the "left") have reservations about the Torah, it behooves those of the "center," who respect all these values, to consider the full panoply of texts and arguments about which the two sides to this question disagree.

The question of whether yeshiva students should be exempt from military service requires the clarification of several points of Jewish law (*halakhah*) and ideology (*machshavah*), such as:

- Torah study offsets everything (*talmud Torah ke-neged kulam*),
- One performing one mitzvah is exempt from another mitzvah (*ha-osek be-mitzvah, patur min ha-mitzvah*),
- Sanctity of the Levites (*kedushat shevet Levi*).
- Mandatory war vs. optional war (*milchemet mitzvah, milchememt ha-reshut*),

We will provide some of the texts that bear upon these points and emphasize their relevance to the question at hand.[1]

* * *

It would be beneficial, at the outset, to consider how this problem arose. We begin, therefore, with the history of the exemption of yeshiva students from the military draft in the State of Israel, followed by the presentation of the relevant legal and philosophical sources, and conclude with a look at the special military-academic arrangement known as Hesder.

Part One: The History of Exemption
1. The War of Independence

---

1. Our secondary sources include: Rabbi Alfred S. Cohen: "On Yeshiva Men Serving in the Army," *Journal of Halacha and Contemporary Society* 23 (1992), 5–31; Rabbi Aharon Lichtenstein: "The Ideology of Hesder," *Tradition* 19/3 (Fall, 1981), 199–217; and Yehezkel Cohen: *Giyyus k'Halakhah* (Jerusalem, 1993).

2. The Establishment of the State of Israel
3. Ben Gurion, the Labor Party, and – especially – the Likud

Part Two: The Halakhic Sources
1. The Importance of Torah study
2. The "Privileged" Status of Levi
3. Mandatory and Optional Wars

Part Three: Practical Conclusions and Considerations
1. The Response of Chief Rabbi Herzog
2. The Hesder Program: Its Evolution and Philosophy

Part One: The History of Exemption
A. THE WAR OF INDEPENDENCE

On March 9, 1948, even before the formal establishment of the state, Israel Galili, chief of staff of the Haganah (acting, apparently, under the instructions of David Ben-Gurion), excused yeshiva students from the compulsory military service that was incumbent upon most other Jews – both men and women. In the Old City of Jerusalem, which was harder pressed for manpower and resources than other parts of the country, some individual yeshiva students volunteered for service, but most refrained on the advice of their yeshiva leaders. For instance:

> It is our Torah opinion that every yeshiva student should know that his rightful place is amongst the army of God. He has no obligation to enlist or to register for any military service whatsoever. (Rav Y.M. Charlap, 1889–1974)
>
> This is our Torah opinion issued as a clear halakhic decision: No yeshiva student who [regularly] occupies the *beit midrash* should enlist or register for anything connected to guard duty, the [military] draft, or the like. It is forbidden to question this [ruling], or to engage in discussion or to make concessions over it, or to seek grounds for latitude even temporarily. (Rav Zvi Pesach Frank, 1873–1960)

Not all the sages (*talmidei chakhamim*) of Jerusalem, however, agreed with this position. Rav Shelomo Yosef Zevin (1888–1978), for instance, wrote in response:

> With all due respect and admiration for the teachers and rabbis, geonim of the Holy City, there is room to ask: Please instruct us; from what source do you derive this conclusion?
>
> Whence do you presume that yeshiva students and *talmidei chakhamim* are exempt from participating in a *milchemet mitzvah* to assist Jews against sworn enemies intent upon their destruction and annihilation, God forbid? Whence do you presume to publicize, in the form of a halakhic decision and *da'at Torah*, that yeshiva students need not register, be counted, report, or anything?

B. THE ESTABLISHMENT OF THE STATE OF ISRAEL

This original exemption was subsequently expanded. According to a report issued by Minister of Defense Shimon Peres, the following were also exempted:

- rabbis of settlements
- rabbis of communities of under 2,000 people
- rabbis serving as supervisors of slaughterhouses in large cities
- rabbis overseeing marriages in large cities
- religious court judges

In the winter of 1948–9, Chief Rabbi Yitzhak Halevi Herzog (1888–1959) requested an extension of the wartime exemption (which is estimated to have affected 400 students at the time), arguing:

> After the terrible Holocaust, in which tens of thousands of yeshiva students were destroyed in Europe – leaving only a pitiful remnant – it is my opinion that they be freed from compulsory military service in order to allow these few to continue the study of our holy Torah, which is also to the glory, and necessity, of our state.

C. BEN-GURION, THE LABOR PARTY AND – ESPECIALLY – THE LIKUD

Ben-Gurion replied to Rabbi Herzog that he would have the Chief of Staff consider the request, which indicated that he did not yet regard this exemption as permanent. In 1949, he sent a confirmation to Rabbi Yitzhak Meir Levin, the (ultra-Orthodox) Agudat Yisrael representative in the Knesset, further indicating that he was motivated by political concerns regarding his governing coalition. In a subsequent meeting with some of the *rashei yeshiva* (including Rabbi Tekochinski and Rabbi Sorotzkin), Ben-Gurion argued that yeshiva students should be given military training in their *yeshivot* – just as Moses and Joshua, according to the Aggadah, were simultaneously Torah leaders and military commanders.

In 1954, the Minister of Defense, Pinhas Lavon, issued orders to draft all yeshiva students who had already been exempted for four years, indicating that the exemption was considered a postponement of service rather than its complete annulment. He was overruled, however, by then Prime Minister Moshe Sharett, after strenuous lobbying by Chief Rabbi Herzog.

In 1957, Ben-Gurion expanded the exemption concept to include Torah teachers as well as students. These teachers were exempted for four years, provided that they taught in private schools (*chadarim*) or community operated schools (*talmudei Torah*). After the fourth year, they were to undergo three months of basic training and could be called for military reserve duty. In 1968, a committee established by Defense Minister Moshe Dayan set the limit of all new Torah related exemptions at 800 a year. This quota remained in effect as long as the Labor Party remained in power.

By 1977, however, when the Likud party came to power with the assistance of coalition agreements with the large ultra-Orthodox (Hareidi) political parties, the total number of exemptions granted had reached 8,257. Defense Ministers Ezer Weizman and Ariel Sharon eliminated the annual quotas and allowed the number of exemptions to rise. By 1985, the number of new exemptions had reached 1,688 and the total number of exemptions stood at 16,011 (nearly double the figure for 1977).[2] In addition, the regulations governing exemptions were relaxed to allow exempted students above the age of 30 to earn money for their teaching. They also granted those above 40 a permanent release from service, rather than the previous postponement.

In 2018, the Defense Ministry produced a proposal that required 3,348 ultra-Orthodox men to enlist in the IDF each year and another 648 would take part in national service (*sheirut le'umi*). These numbers would increase by eight percent each year for three years, then 6.5 percent for another three years, and finally by five percent for four more years, reaching 5,737 ultra-Orthodox military recruits and 1,107 national servicemen after a decade.[3]

Part Two: The Halakhic Sources

A. THE IMPORTANCE OF TORAH STUDY:

The paramount importance of Torah study is stated explicitly in the well-known Mishnah in *Pei'ah* (1:1): "Torah study is equal to all of them [*mitzvot*]."

Maimonides also gave exceptional emphasis to the preeminence of Torah study:

2.

	1948	1988
Total Jewish population	600,000	3,660,000
Number of exemptions	400	18,800
Percentage of exemptions	.07%	.5%

If the percentage of exemptions granted in 1988 had remained at the level of 1948, the total number in 1988 would have been only 2,500. By 1998, the estimated number of current exemptions was 30,000.

3. *The Times of Israel*, Feb. 1, 2021. https://www.timesofisrael.com/idf-exemption-for-haredim-expires-but-nothings-likely-to-change-for-now/

A man is commanded to be fruitful and multiply but a woman is not. He becomes liable for the performance of this mitzvah from the age of seventeen, and if he reaches the age of twenty without marrying, he has transgressed and annulled a positive commandment. If he is preoccupied with Torah study, however, and forgoes marriage because the need to make a living would intrude on his Torah study, then he is permitted to tarry because one who is engaged in the performance of one mitzvah is exempt from another and most certainly [one engaged in] Torah study. (*Hilkhot Ishut* 15:2)

Indeed, no less a figure of authority than Joshua is chastised in a talmudic passage for allowing Torah study to be suspended. While he was on the outskirts of Jericho (5:13 ff.), he was approached by a sword-bearing figure who identified himself as "a captain of the hosts [*sar tzeva'*] of the Lord," and who informed him that "I have come now." The Talmud elaborates:

> He [the captain] said: Yesterday, you suspended the afternoon daily [*tamid*] sacrifice and now you have suspended Torah study! [Joshua] asked: Over which have you come [to rebuke me]? He said: "I have come now" [i.e., the latter]. Immediately, Joshua spent that night in the valley. R. Yohanan said: He spent it [immersed] in the depths of *halakhah* [i.e., in Torah study]. (*Megillah* 3a)

Elsewhere, Maimonides elaborated on this principle and declared:

> No mitzvah whatsoever is equivalent to Torah study. Rather, Torah study offsets all the other *mitzvot* because study leads to [proper] action. Therefore, study always takes precedence over action. If confronted with [either] the performance of a mitzvah or Torah study, if the mitzvah can be performed by others – one should not interrupt his study. Otherwise, let him perform the mitzvah and then resume studying. (*Talmud Torah* 3:3–4)

B. RESOLVING A CONTRADICTION IN MAIMONIDES

Is this not a contradiction? On one hand, Maimonides said that Torah study is inviolable, while, on the other hand, he stipulated that it is permissible to suspend Torah study for the performance of a mitzvah that will otherwise go unfulfilled. The Me'iri (Provence, 13th century) spoke to this point, saying:

> Even though one who is occupied with a mitzvah is exempt from another mitzvah, this does not apply to Torah study. Since its essence is to understand the fulfillment of the other *mitzvot*, it is itself suspended for the sake of [the performance] of any mitzvah that cannot be fulfilled by another. (*Beit ha-Bechirah, Moed Katan* 9b)

In other words, since the purpose of Torah study is primarily utilitarian, that is, to make the proper performance of other *mitzvot* possible, the latter have priority and Torah study must yield to them.

If that is the case, why distinguish between *mitzvot*? Torah study should yield before all other mitzvot, regardless of whether others can fulfill them. The answer is that "Torah" faced a dilemma. On one hand, if it provided an exemption for its students from all other *mitzvot*, it would be undermining the very cause of Torah study, which is the performance of those *mitzvot*. But, if it required its students to interrupt their study for the performance of every single mitzvah, it is conceivable that there would never be sufficient time for study and, as a result, performance itself would suffer.

The resolution of this dilemma was not to create a blanket exemption, but a limited one. Only mitzvot that would find no other fulfillment take precedence over Torah study; other *mitzvot* may be left to others to fulfill.

Another approach is to distinguish between temporary and permanent interruptions. Reading the Megillah and blowing the *shofar* (to cite the examples used in *Megillah* 3a–b) take up a finite and limited amount of time; therefore, Torah study can be interrupted for them and resumed thereafter. Making a living – specifically because of marriage – on the other hand, can be an ongoing concern leading to continuous interruption of Torah study. The temporary suspension is tolerable, while the permanent, according to some, is not.

C. THE "PRIVILEGED" STATUS OF *B'NEI TORAH*: LEARNING FROM LEVI

The exemption of Torah students from military service is frequently compared to that of the tribe of Levi. Let us see what that entailed and whether the cases are comparable.

The source of this distinctive status is the Torah's exclusion of Levi from the census of the Jewish nation, which was designed to address military service (Numbers 1:3). Rashbam, for one, concluded: "The reason [for the exclusion] is that they are not subject to military service" (v. 16).

Maimonides formulated the "privileged" status of Levi as follows:

> Why did the tribe of Levi not share in the Land of Israel and its spoils with his brother tribes? Because he was set apart to serve God and instruct His proper ways and just laws to the public... Therefore, the Levites were kept apart from the mundane. They neither conduct war – like the remainder of Israel – nor do they inherit land, nor acquire anything personal by way of force. Rather, they are God's army... and He provides for them....
>
> Not only the tribe of Levi, but any individual in the world who volunteers – of his own volition – to devote himself to God's service and knowledge, and who casts off the yoke of the many concerns people ordinarily have, becomes sanctified. He is devoted, eternally, to God, and God will make provision for his needs as He does for the Priests and Levites. (*Shemittah ve-Yoveil* 13:12–13)

For obvious reasons, the military exemption of yeshiva students remained a purely theoretical question until the Israeli War of Independence. The analogous question of exemption from communal taxation, however, was dealt with by religious authorities (poskim).

The *Terumat ha-Deshen* (Israel Isserlein, 1390–1460), for one, treated it restrictively:

> The masses are not of the opinion to exempt a scholar [from the payment of communal taxes] unless he is the head of a yeshiva, and even this [exemption] is only in Austria... [where] it is a widespread custom not to tax the head of a yeshiva... In Germany, however, it appears to me that it was not customary to exempt scholars... because it requires great punctiliousness to resume one's scholarship upon release from other considerations and nowadays people are not so exacting. (Responsa #342)

Rabbi Moses Isserles (the "Rema," 16th century), however, treated the issue more broadly, indicating that a Torah scholar would be exempt:

> It does not matter whether one attends a yeshiva or only that he is reputed to be a scholar.... As far as tax exemption is concerned, we are not that picky providing he is a reputable scholar. (*Yoreh Dei'ah* 253:2)

D. THE IMPLICATIONS

From Maimonides's equation of the Levites with "any individual in the world"[4] who undertakes a life of sacred devotion, combined with the Rema's lack of distinction between a rosh yeshiva and an ordinary scholar, the conclusion may be drawn that all yeshiva students are likewise exempt from military service. Hence, Rabbi Eliezer Waldenberg ruled:

---

4. Hebrew: *kol 'ish va-'ish mi-kol ba'ei 'olam*; an unusual locution, made even more striking due to its location. Rambam regularly used the concluding *halakhah* of one of the fourteen constitutent sections of the *Mishneh Torah* to espouse a broad philosophical principle. *Hilkhot Shemittah ve-Yoveil* concludes *Sefer Zera'im*.

Of this sort of Torah scholars (i.e., for whom Torah is truly a vocation and who have voluntarily cast off the yoke of the many concerns that people ordinarily bear), one can say that it is universally acknowledged that they are exempt from participating in battle and from all military service – including a mandatory war – because they are God's army and are entitled to be freed from mundane concerns while they are focused on the creative soul of the nation. (*Hilkhot Medinah*, volume 2 [Jerusalem, 1952], 62)

Rav Aharon Lichtenstein, on the other hand, ruled in line with the more restrictive ruling of the *Terumat ha-Deshen*:

Even if we grant that the Rambam's statement does imply a categorical dispensation in purely halakhic terms, it remains of little practical significance. We have yet to examine just to whom it applies. A Levi is defined genealogically. Those who are equated with him, however, literally or symbolically, are defined by spiritual qualities, and for these the Rambam sets a very high standard indeed... To how large a segment of the Torah community... does this lofty typology apply? To two percent? Five percent? Can anyone... confront a mirror and tell himself that he ought not to go to the army because he is kodesh kodashim, sanctum sanctorum, in the Rambam's terms?[5]

E. MANDATORY AND OPTIONAL WAR

Rabbi Waldenberg's emphasis on "including a mandatory war," however, is not explicit in the Maimonidean passage he cited. Where does it originate? To answer this question, we must first define the categories of war and why they should influence the question of whether Torah students are exempt.

The distinction between types of war is introduced in the Mishnah:

---

5. "On the Ideology of Hesder" *Tradition* (Fall 1981), p. 212.

> Where do [these exemptions] apply? In optional wars [*reshut*]. However, in mandatory wars [*mitzvah*] everyone must serve, including a groom straight from his chamber and a bride from her canopy. R. Yehudah says: This applies to a mandatory war, but in a compulsory war [*chovah*], everyone must serve... (*Sotah* 44b)

The Talmud clarified the distinction between the categories of R. Yehudah and those of the Sages as follows:

> R. Yohanan says: The "optional" war of the Sages is "mandatory" to R. Yehudah, and "mandatory" of the Sages is "compulsory" to R. Yehudah. Rava says: Everyone agrees that Joshua's wars of conquest were compulsory and that David's wars of [territorial] expansion were optional. They differ in regard to preventing foreign invasion. One calls this mandatory, while the other calls it optional. What practical difference does it make? To the [principle of] "One who is engaged in a mitzvah is exempt from [another] mitzvah." (Ibid.)

Maimonides codified this distinction as follows:

> The first war a king undertakes must be a mandatory war. Which war is mandatory? The war against the seven [Canaanite] nations, against Amalek, and in defense of Jews against enemy attack. Subsequently, he may launch an optional war, such as a war undertaken to expand the borders of Israel or to enhance his fame and reputation. (*Hilkhot Melakhim* 5:1)

The position of Rav Zevin (see part I, section 1), i.e., that yeshiva students should not be exempted from the War of Independence since it was a mandatory war, is validated by Maimonides as well:

> In which circumstances do we grant leave from military service? In an optional war [*reshut*], but in a mandatory war [*milchemet mitzvah*] everyone serves, even a groom... and a bride... (*Hilkhot Melakhim* 7:4)

F. AN ENLIGHTENING HISTORICAL PRECEDENT

Rabbi Abraham Isaac ha-Kohen Kook, later to become the first Ashkenazi Chief Rabbi of Palestine under the British Mandate, was in Europe when World War I broke out and spent part of the war in London. While there, his opinion was solicited concerning the drafting of yeshiva students into the British army. His reply concluded:

> Therefore, scholars who are engaged with Torah are defending the land and assisting the national war effort no less – and even more – than active soldiers. It is therefore a certain conclusion that an idealistic kingdom that recognizes the splendor of sanctity will not force students who diligently enter the portals of Torah to nullify their Torah study in order to undertake physical activities for which they are unqualified.[6]

However, when this corespondence was cited in 1948 in support of an unqualified exemption for yeshiva students from military service in the fledgling State of Israel, Rabbi Zvi Yehudah Kook, Rav Kook's son, was irate. He even went to the length of having the following broadsdide, dated 25 Nisan 5708, posted on the streets of Jerusalem:

> I have seen publicized throughout Jerusalem a fragment of a letter from my father, purporting that he supported – God forbid – the evasion of the full responsibility to defend us and the entire Jewish community. I am obliged to give notice, for the sake of the truth of Torah, that he wrote this letter in Adar of 5677 (1917) in London in an effort to free scholars from the war between England, Russia, and Germany, in which there was no obligation of saving Jewish lives or the Land of Israel.... We must lament the use of this fragment of his holy letter, ignoring the context it treats, and publicly implying that

---

6. Rabbi A.I. Kook, *Correspondences* (*Iggerot ha-Rayah*) III Jerusalem (1965), #810, pp. 89–92. This correspondence is dealt with substantially by Neriyah Gutel: "Deferment or Draft for Yeshiva Students?" (Hebrew) *Amadot* 1 (2010), 25 ff.

it has any relevance to our current situation, for it is akin to the worst and most shameful kind of deception....[7]

Part Three: Practical Conclusions and Considerations
A. THE RESPONSUM OF CHIEF RABBI HERZOG

Based on these distinctions, Rabbi Yitzhak Halevi Herzog, the first Chief Ashkenazi Rabbi of the State of Israel, composed a responsum on 16 Tevet, 5708 (December 29, 1947), in which he clarified the halakhic status of the military exemption for yeshiva students. He made six points concerning the involvement of yeshiva students in the ongoing War of Independence:

> The War of Independence is most assuredly a mandatory war (*milchemet mitzvah*) requiring universal participation. This specifically includes yeshiva students on the analogy of Joshua's original war of conquest (according to *Eiruvin* 54b, all Jews at that time were scholars), and the wars of the Hasmoneans, to whom we refer, liturgically, as "engaged in Torah study" (*'oskei Toratekha*).
>
> The war is being waged to save the Yishuv (settlement) and the many Holocaust survivors who had found refuge there. It is a shame that so many Torah giants declined to see the opportunity to establish an independent Jewish state as the commencement of the final redemption (*'atchalta' dige'ulah*).
>
> There is no halakhic source for exempting yeshiva students from the fundamental obligation of saving lives (*hatzalat nefashot*). The oft-cited ruling of the Radvaz (Responsa 3:627) – that one need not place himself in potential danger even to rescue another from definite danger – applies only on an individual basis, not a national one.

---

7. Z.Y. Kook, *Public Law* (*Hilkhot Tzibbur*) 1 (Jerusalem, 1987), 13. Cited by Gutel, *op. cit.*

When both parties are endangered, there is unquestionably an obligation to provide rescue. In his words: "How can anyone say, let Shimon stand guard and fight to protect himself and Reuven, while Reuven sits by idly at Shimon's expense because Reuven is a yeshiva student?"

There is no foundation for the complete exemption of yeshiva students from a mandatory war. Rather, care must be exercised to insure the continuation of Torah study. In the current situation, the leaders of the Yishuv are sensitive to the special needs of the yeshiva students and willing to arrive at an appropriate arrangement with them. Such an arrangement (*hesder*) would require the enlistment of some students and the exemption of others.

Participation in the military would be beneficial to the yeshivot themselves, while failure to participate would only stir animosity. Previously, even *kibbutzim* would (grudgingly) recognize the value of Torah study; the abject refusal of Torah students to join the army – even in the critical case of the Old City of Jerusalem – would alienate and antagonize them.

Rabbi Herzog compared the sacrifice Torah students would make to the sacrifices offered on the altar and reminded his readers how sensitive the Sages were that no slander should attach itself to the altar (*Gittin* 55b).

The key term, here, is "arrangement" (*hesder*, see below), which inspired a new approach to the combination of military service and yeshiva study.

B. *HESDER*: ITS EVOLUTION AND PHILOSOPHY

In 1957, Deputy Minister of Religious Affairs, Dr. Zerah Warhaftig, received the following memo from the national administration of the B'nai Akiva religious Zionist youth movement:

> The problem of the enlistment of yeshiva students is thwarting the development of our own yeshivot, particularly Kerem

b'Yavneh.... Our students are not willing, for any consideration, to escape military service on the grounds that they are yeshiva students. This stands in absolute opposition to their national consciousness and social awareness. As a result, even those who would devote several years to Torah study are confronted with the problem of military service.

For these reasons, we have decided, after consultation with several rashei yeshiva and educators, to enter negotiations with the security establishment in order to find a solution. Our recommendation concerns the B'nai Akiva yeshivot: Kerem b'Yavneh, Torah u'Melakhah, and Merkaz haRav... We assume that Yeshivat haDarom will also participate...[8]

This recommendation, if accepted, will open before us broad horizons and will enable us to fashion a type of student-scholar (*talmid chakham*) who is spiritually whole and able to serve as a true educational role model to his pupils.

The result of this recommendation was the initiation, by order of the Minister of Defense, of the Hesder program that combined military service with yeshiva study along the lines of the existing Nachal service (*No'ar Chalutzi Locheim*) that combined military service and pioneering, agricultural work. This arrangement allowed these yeshiva students to continue their Torah study while fulfilling their national responsibilities. Hesder students have served the Israel Defense Forces in many ranks and capacities and have achieved wide recognition for their contributions to the state. They also continue to

---

8. According to his official biography on the website of Yeshivat Har Etzion, Rabbi Yehuda Amital conceived of the Hesder program while serving as head of Yeshivat HaDarom in Rehovot (http://etzion.org.il/vbm/archive/ramim.html). It is particularly noteworthy that Rav Amital himself enlisted in the Hagganah on May 15, 1948, even though it was Shabbat, relying upon the sanction of the Chief Rabbinate. See Elyashiv Reichner: *By Faith Alone; the Story of Rabbi Yehuda Amital* (Jerusalem: Maggid, 2011), 139.

serve their communities and yeshivot as teachers, rabbis, judges and even as *rashei yeshiva*.

In the years 1981–83, while approximately 1,400 yeshiva students were being granted exemptions each year (these were the very years in which the number of total exemptions was growing – as we have described above), an average of 400 yeshiva students were enlisting, annually, in Hesder. In 1984 – with the number of exemptions still around 1,400 – there were over 700 such enlistments. In 1991, the Hesder program was awarded the prestigious Israel Prize for its contributions to Israeli society. As of 2011, there were 68 Hesder *yeshivot* in Israel with an combined enrollment of over 8,000 students and the number has grown considerably since then.

Overall, Hesder students are greatly overrepresented in combat units (80% enlistment versus an average of 30% for other inductees) offsetting the relatively limited time they spend in military service (16 months vs. 36).[9]

C. THE PHILOSOPHY OF HESDER

In 1981, Rav Aharon Lichtenstein, *rosh yeshiva* of Har Etzion, published a lengthy and eloquent statement on the philosophy of Hesder *yeshivot*. First, Rav Lichtenstein emphasized the nature of the "arrangement" inherent in the concept of Hesder:

> Hence, to the extent that the term Hesder, "arrangement," connotes an accommodation arrived at between conflicting sides, it is somewhat of a misnomer. Hesder is not the result of a compromise between the respective positions of Roshe Yeshivah and the Ministry of Defense. It is rather a compromise with reality. We do occasionally argue with the generals over details and they do not always sufficiently appreciate the preeminence of the spiritual factor. The basic concern with

---

9. See the 2014 study conducted by Dr. Benny Porat of the *Israel Democracy Institute:* https://en.idi.org.il/articles/6526

security, however, is ours no less than theirs. ("The Ideology of Hesder," *Tradition* 19/3, 202)

Rav Lichtenstein elaborated on what he saw as the advantages of Hesder – both civic and ideological – to a yeshiva high-school graduate. First, the civic advantages:

> The advantages, judged from a student's perspective, are fairly clear. Most obviously, the tour of actual army service is shorter. While a student is tied down by Hesder for almost five years, he only spends, unless he becomes an officer, about sixteen months in uniform. Most important, however, Hesder provides a convenient framework for discharging two different – and to some extent conflicting – obligations. It enables him, morally and psychologically, to salve both his religious and his national conscience by sharing in the collective defense burden without cutting himself off from the matrix of Torah. Socially – and this of course has religious implications as well – Hesder offers him a desirable context as, even while in the army, he will often be stationed with fellow Hesder-niks. And Hesder enables him, pragmatically, to keep his future academic and vocational options open. Unlike his peers at non-Hesder *yeshivot*, he can, upon completing the Hesder program, legally pursue any course of study and/or employment within the mainstream of Israeli society. (p. 200)

The ideological advantages, however, were no less important:

> Optimally, Hesder does not merely provide a religious cocoon for young men fearful of being contaminated by the potentially secularizing influences of general army life – although it incidentally serves this need as well. Hesder at its finest seeks to attract and develop *bnei torah* who are profoundly motivated by the desire to become serious *talmidei hakhamim* but who concurrently feel morally and religiously bound to help defend

their people and their country; who, given the historical exigencies of their time and place, regard this dual commitment as both a privilege and a duty; who, in comparison with their non-Hesder confreres love not (to paraphrase Byron's Childe Harold) Torah less but Israel more. It provides a context within which students can focus upon enhancing their personal spiritual and intellectual growth while yet heeding the call to public service, and it thus enables them to maintain an integrated Jewish existence. (pp. 200–1)

Postscript

Over the past several years, the status of the yeshiva exemption has increasingly become a proverbial "hot potato," tossed about cavalierly – perhaps even cynically – during negotiations over coalition politics in Israel. Whenever a governing coalition can be formed without Hareidi participation, the proposed law gets ratified; when the pendulum swings back and Hareidim are wooed for their Knesset votes, it gets rescinded. Partisan politics aside, however, it may be possible to make a principled pronouncement on the value of military service for Torah scholars based on a comment of Maimonides.

In the fall of 1195 (possibly 1196), Maimonides composed the first of several letters that he despatched to the Jewish sages of Provence in France. Unlike most of his correspondence, which he undertook in his native Arabic, this letter was written in Hebrew because Arabic was not widely understood among its intended recipients. While its subject, at large, is astrology, it contains the following poignant observation:

> This is the cause of the loss of our sovereignty and the destruction of our Temple and their consequences that affect us to this very day. "Our ancestors erred; but they have since disappeared [yet we suffer the consequences of their error]." They found many works in the field of astrology – matters that comprise the essence of idolatry, as we have explained in the "Laws of

Idolatry" – that caused them to err and to be misled, believing them to be sophisticated sciences and possessed of great utility. [Therefore,] they chose not to engage in the study of war or conquest, imagining that these [astrological] matters were decisive, on account of which the prophets refered to them as fools and simpletons. They truly were foolish, suckered by useless ineffectuality.[10]

In other words, Maimonides stipulated that military knowledge and experience have a considerable value and, indeed, that they are indispensable for the successful conduct of affairs of state. Bearing in mind that the letter is addressed to Torah sages, it is difficult to escape the implication that he would regard military training for Torah students a prerequisite for the maintenance of a Jewish state.[11]

---

10. Yitzhak Shilat, *Ig'rot ha-Rambam* vol. II (Jerusalem, 1995), 478. In another of these letters – addressed to the sages of Lunel – Maimonides stated that the torch of Torah scholarship, then flickering throughout the Muslim world, would soon be passed to the sages of Provence.
11. This very point is reiterated by Rabbi Dr. Eliezer Berkovitz in "Knowledge of the World and Knowledge of God," a 1962 essay advocating the combination of Judaic and general studies in Jewish education. Idem: *Essential Essays on Judaism* (Jerusalem: Shalem Press, 2002), 237.

Acquiring Land in Eretz Yisrael
The *Makhpeilah* Cave, Joseph's Tomb, and the Temple Mount

Preface

The common denominator uniting the three places in the title of this essay is suggested by the Midrash in *Bereishit Rabbah* (79:7):

> R. Yudan ben R. Shimon said: This is one of the three places about which the nations of the world cannot taunt Israel, saying: "You have stolen them!" They are the Tomb of the Patriarchs, the Temple Mount, and Joseph's Tomb.[1]

The Tomb of the Patriarchs

The Torah (Genesis 23) tells us how Abraham purchased a field and a cave in Hebron to serve as Sarah's final resting-place. Uncharacteristically, the text dwells on every slight detail of the sale, including verbatim transcripts of Abraham's conversations with the local population (*benei Cheit*, the Hittites) and the owner of the field (Ephron).

Our opening question was posed by Malbim: "Of what halakhic or other traditional significance is this entire story?" Ibn Ezra also

---

1. As is well-known, the theme of the proprietary rights of the People of Israel to the Land of Israel is struck by Rashi in his commentary to very first verse in the Torah. The fact that this challenge is still being issued 1,000 years later speaks volumes.

recognized that the Torah's attention here to even minute detail (v. 17, for instance, takes note of the trees in the field) reflects an extraordinary significance, and he explained (as though in answer to Malbim's question) that: "This episode was reported to inform us of the superiority of Eretz Yisrael above all other countries."

A. THE DIALOGUE

Let us analyze the entire course of the transaction by copying out the dialogue in parallel columns, one, what Abraham said, and the other: how the Hittites, or Ephron, responded. For example:

Abraham	Hittites; Ephron
I am a resident-alien among you	You are a divine prince in our midst
Grant me a perpetual gravesite among you	In the choicest gravesite you may bury your dead
So I may bury my dead	Not one of us will withhold his gravesite from you
Let him [Ephron] grant me his Makhpelah cave at the edge of his field... Let him sell it to me at full price...as a perpetual gravesite.	I have given you the field and the cave within it I have granted you...I have given it to you to bury your dead.

Note Abraham's opening declaration: "I am a resident-alien (*geir ve-toshav*) in your midst." Is this just an expression of humility (to which the Hittites respond by saying, "Oh, no! You're a prince of a man!"), or does it contain very specific legal implications?

Compare this verse:

> Land can never be sold in perpetuity, for it belongs entirely to Me; you are only resident-aliens (*geirim ve-toshavim*) in it (Leviticus 25:23).

What is the similarity between our status vis-à-vis God and Abraham's status regarding the Hittites? Just as we can own land only up to the Jubilee year, but not forever, because we are only "resident-aliens" before God, so Abraham could not – ordinarily – own a perpetual cave-tomb in Hebron because, legally, he was only a "resident-alien" – and not a full-fledged citizen – before the Hittites.

B. INDIRECTION

The *Pa'ane'ach Raza'* (13th century) asked a significant question regarding Abraham's conversation with the local population:

> It is difficult [to understand]: Why did Abraham not speak directly to Ephron instead of first turning to the Hittites?

We might add to his question: Why did Abraham show the Hittites such respect, even bowing down to them twice?

Perhaps Abraham spoke to them directly, and respectfully, because he needed their public permission to purchase the field in perpetuity before approaching Ephron to negotiate the sale. As the Chizkuni (France, 13th century) wrote (v. 7):

> Abraham needed them all. Even had Ephron sold him the field, he would not have been permitted to use it as a cemetery without public permission.

Sa'adiah Gaon (882–942) surmised that the Hittites had what we would call "zoning laws" restricting the use of private land for such uncongenial purposes as a cemetery, like the talmudic laws of *bar meitzra*. Abraham was seeking public approval for a "zoning variance."[2]

Joseph's Tomb

As Jacob returned from Aram to the Land of Israel, he encountered his brother Esav, who along with 400 men had come to intercept him

---

2. For additional details, or alternate approaches, see: Nehama Leibowitz: *Iyyunim be-Seifer Bereishit* "Chayyei Sarah" (1), 207–213.

(Gen. 32–33). As Rashi observed (32:9), Jacob equipped himself for this fateful encounter in a threefold fashion: sending gifts, introspection and prayer, and military preparations.

Jacob emerged successfully from this encounter and arrived at the city of Shechem in a manner the Torah calls *shaleim* (33:18), "whole" or "unscathed." In order to commemorate his safe return, he did two things: he purchased his campsite (v. 19) and there he raised a monument (v. 20).

A. WHAT IS THE SIGNIFICANCE OF THIS PURCHASE?

On one hand, it is possible (perhaps even likely) that Jacob's purpose was personal and immediate: to mark his return to the land he was to inherit, by actually acquiring part of it, or, alternatively, to finally have a place to call his own. On the other hand, our commentators saw a great symbolic significance in this acquisition. Ibn Ezra, for instance, commented: "Scripture reveals this to inform us that there is exceptional superiority to Eretz Yisrael," and Ramban remarked: "In any event, this deed alludes to the future."

To what future event did Ramban allude?[3] Is it a specific event in the history of Israel, or does it symbolize all future land purchases in Eretz Yisrael? What is the "exceptional superiority" to which Ibn Ezra refered? Remember that we quoted Ibn Ezra (above) as saying: "To inform us of the superiority of Eretz Yisrael above all other countries." Is Eretz Yisrael superior in and of itself? Or, does it acquire its superiority from the Jewish people who invest their lives, hopes, and resources in it?

Hundreds of years later, the bones of Joseph – which were especially preserved and carried out of Egypt during the Exodus – were put to rest in this very same field:

---

3. The theme of ancestral deeds portending those of their descendants (*ma'aseh avot, siman la-banim*), which is struck here by Ramban, is treated by Nehama Leibowitz in *Iyyunim be-Seifer Bereishit* "VaYishlach" (5), 253–269, and by Ayalah Levi-Feldblum in *Ma'ayanot* 11 (1985), 74–83.

> And the bones of Joseph which the Israelites took out of Egypt they buried in Shechem in the field that Jacob bought from the sons of Hamor, father of Shechem, for one hundred coins, and it became the inheritance of Joseph's sons (Joshua 24:32).

A comparison between this verse in Joshua and other verses from Genesis and Exodus that refer to the preservation and and transportation of Joseph's bones, is noteworthy:

> Genesis 50:26: "They embalmed him, and he was placed in a sarcophagus in Egypt."

> Exodus 13:9: "Moses took Joseph's bones along with him."

It might be worthwhile to add Rashi's observation on the similarity between Jacob's instructions regarding his burial, and those of Joseph, which we find in his commentary on Gen. 48:22:

> Since you [Joseph] are trying to take care of my burial, I am giving you a hereditary burial plot. Where? In Shechem.

Temple Mount

In 2 Samuel chapter 24, we read how King David violated Torah law in the conduct of a census, and how God offered him a choice of three alternate forms of punishment: seven years of famine, three months of military setbacks, or three days of plague. David chose the plague, replying to the prophet with the phrase in the siddur that now introduces *Tachanun*:

> And David said to Gad: I am greatly distressed. Let me fall into the Lord's hands – for his compassion is exceeding – and into human hands, let me not fall (v. 14).[4]

---

4. There is a disagreement among the exegetes whether David sinned in the manner of the census (i.e., counting directly rather than by soliciting

The ensuing plague struck, killing seventy thousand people. When it reached Jerusalem, however, God revoked the evil decree and cancelled the plague. It stopped at the threshing floor (*goren*) of Aravna, a non-Jewish resident of the city. To completely terminate the plague, David sought to purchase the threshing floor, to build an altar there and offer sacrifices.

Aravna consented. The purchase was made, the altar was built, and the sacrifices offered. The plague ended (and so does the book of Samuel).

A. REPETITION

In 1 Chronicles, chapter 21, there is a replay of the story, and it is with that retelling of the purchase that we shall deal here, since it provides a distinct and tangible link to one of the previous purchases: the language that Chronicles uses to describe the negotiations between David and Aravna.[5]

B. COMPARISON

By comparing the transaction between David and Aravna (according to 1 Chron. 21:22–26) to the story of Abraham's purchase of the tomb of the patriarchs (Genesis 23), we will demonstrate that the later story was consciously and deliberately patterned after the earlier one.

---

half-shekels, cf. Rashi on Exodus 30:11), or whether his sin was in the very act of an unnecessary counting (cf. Nahmanides, Numbers 1:3).

5. In Chronicles, he is called "Arnan." Neither Aravna nor Arnan is a proper name, but a title, the Hurian word for "chieftain," and that is why they sometimes appear in Tanakh with the definite article (2 Samuel 24:16), something not done with proper names.

Comparisons between earlier and later books of Tanakh are simplified using Abba Bendavid, *Makbilot ba-Mikra* (Jerusalem: CARTA).

Abraham and the Hittites (Gen. 22)	David and the Jebusites (1 Chr. 21)
Introduce me to Ephron…let him give me the cave	David said to Arnan: Give me the granary
He will give it to me for the full price (*kesef malei'*)	Give it to me for a full price (*kesef malei'*)
Ephron replied, saying: I have given you the field	Arnan replied: Take it
[Abraham] said to Ephron: Take the money	David said to Arnan: I will surely pay full price
Abraham weighed out the 400 silver coins to Ephron	David gave Arnan the 600 silver coins
There he buried Sarah	There he built an altar

Jerusalem, between Jews and Muslims

While Jewish settlement in the Land of Israel was variously interrupted by Babylonians, Greeks, Romans, Persians, Arabs, Crusaders, Mongols and Turks, it is the continued Arab-Muslim presence in Jerusalem and its regard for that city that lie at the root of ongoing violence that has been directed by Arab extremists towards Jews throughout the State of Israel.

The following is offered in consideration of the likelihood that once the subject of Jerusalem is introduced, it is difficult to close the conversation before referring to its contemporary political, religious and symbolic significance. While the sources we provide here do not deal with the rival Jewish and Muslim claims to Jerusalem, per se, they do offer an unusual insight into the importance both religions attach to what Jews call the "Temple Mount" (*Har haBayit*), and Muslims call the "Noble Sanctuary" (*al-Haram al-Sharif*).

The Historical Background

From the time of the destruction of the Second Temple until the beginning of the seventh century, the Land of Israel was part of the Roman-Byzantine empires. While Jews continued to live in Israel, they were forbidden to live in Jerusalem. From 614–629, however, Israel was ruled once again by the Persians, and then briefly retaken by the Byzantine emperor Heraclius, until it was finally conquered by the Arabs/Muslims, under the Caliph Omar in 638.

This last conquest was decidedly favorable to the Jews, who actively supported and assisted the Arab conquerors. As a result of this cooperation, and on the background of Muhammad's adoption of many Jewish principles and beliefs, the resettlement of Jews in Jerusalem was actually one of the terms of surrender imposed by Omar on the Patriarch Sophronius, leader of the conquered Christian community. Indeed, a document discovered in the Cairo Genizah reports that seventy Jewish families from Tiberias were allowed to settle in the southern part of Jerusalem, where they were employed in cleaning and leveling the Temple Mount.

Their community grew and flourished, and in the eighth century Jews were among those who guarded the walls of the Dome of the Rock (commonly, if erroneously, called the Mosque of Omar). In Hebron, too, Jewish support of the Muslim conquest was rewarded. Jews were extended the protection of the authorities and were permitted to build a synagogue at the entrance to the cave of the Patriarchs (*me'arat ha-makhpeilah*).

The Sources

Two sources, one Muslim and the other Jewish, deal with the status of the Temple Mount during that important transitional period. The former acknowledges a Muslim debt to earlier Jewish tradition concerning the location of the Temple Mount, while the latter recognizes Islam for its benevolent treatment of Judaism, in general, and Jerusalem, in particular.

A. OMAR IN JERUSALEM

The Caliph Omar wished to celebrate his successful conquest of Jerusalem by establishing a place of prayer there – a mosque (in Arabic: *masgad*, related to *sagid*, the Aramaic word for "bowing"). In order to determine its best location, he summoned a trusted lieutenant, an apostate Jew named Ka'b al-Achbar (Hebrew: *chaver*), who had converted to Islam. Ka'b recommended the site of the "Temple Rock," probably the "foundation stone" (*'even ha-shetiyah*), which Omar rejected as too "Jewish." Instead, he ordered the mosque prepared at the southern end of the Temple Mount, the site of today's al-Aksa mosque:

> When Omar came to Jerusalem he said: "Bring me Ka'b!" and Omar asked him: "Where do you think we should put the place of prayer?" Ka'b answered: "By the Temple rock." Omar said: "By God, Ka'b, you are following after Judaism; I saw you take off your sandals." Ka'b replied: "I wanted to feel the touch of it with my bare feet."
>
> "I saw you," said Omar, "[However,] we were not commanded concerning the rock, but we were commanded concerning the Ka'aba in Mecca."
>
> So, Omar made the forepart [of the Temple Mount] into the prayer place. Then Omar went up from the place where he had prayed, to the heap of garbage in which the Romans had hidden the Temple in the time of the children of Israel. And Omar said to the people: "Do as I do" and he knelt by the heap and knelt on the fold of his cloak [in prayer].[1]

---

1. Bernard Lewis: *Islam*, vol. II (New York: Harper & Row, 1974), p. 3. Beginning in the fourth century, the Christians of Jerusalem, were accustomed to deposit garbage and rubble on the Temple Mount. Omar had it removed in order to clear the site for building the Mosque of al-Aksa. Curiously, a later Sephardic Jewish folktale substituted the Ottoman Sultan Suleiman the Magnificent (sixteenth century) for Omar, and had him order the Christians of Bethlehem to remove the garbage in order to expose the portion of the retaining wall of the Temple that we know as the *kotel*. The Dome of the Rock was built over 50 years later (691) by the Ummayyad Caliph Abd al-Malik. Its popular, but erroneous attribution to Omar was due, in large part, to the incident described here.

B. *NISTAROT SHEL RABBI SHIMʻON BAR YOCHAI*

The frequent and catastrophic changes in the balance of world power in the seventh century (Byzantium-Persia-Islam) struck many contemporary observers as the fulfillment of the prophecy regarding Gog and Magog (Ezekiel 38–39), that is, a battle that was supposed to preceed the Messianic age. The many similarities between Judaism and the new religion of Islam, the positive attitude that the early Caliphs took toward their Jewish subjects, and the renewed interest – and settlement – in Jerusalem, all left their mark on this eighth-century Midrash, which purports to be a dialogue between R. Shimʻon and the angel Metatron.

> Said R. Shimʻon: "How will salvation come at the hands of the Yishmaelim [Muslims]?" Said Metatron: "God will provide them with a prophet [Muhammad] who will conquer the land [of Israel] for them. They will rebuild ruined cities, clear the roads, plant gardens and orchards and return the land to you vastly improved....
>
> Then the second King of Yishmael [Omar] will conquer all the empires. He will come to Jerusalem and worship there [see the previous text]. He will fight the Edomim [Christians] who will flee before him.... He will be a friend of Israel. He will seal the breaches in the walls [of Israel's cities] and the breaches of the Temple. He will clear off Mount Moriah, level it off entirely, and build a Temple." Had the Jews been worthy, the scion of David [Messiah] would have arisen immediately, at the start of the kingdom of Yishmael. Since they were unworthy, however, he will not come until the end of their kingdom.[2]

---

2. Judah Even-Shmuel, *Midreshei Geʼulah* (Jerusalem, 1954), 188–190.

The Azharot of Rav Sa'adiah Gaon
An Exercise in *Ta'amei HaMitzvot*

Preface

Although the biblical phrase *'aseret hadib'rot* is usually translated as "Ten Commandments," that is a misnomer.[1] If the tablets recorded commandments (which are properly refered to, in Hebrew, as *mitzvot*) there are more than ten, and the very first of them is hardly a commandment at all, but a declaration. Our purpose here, however, is to show that, according to Sa'adiah Gaon, these are really ten broad categories within which all 613 *mitzvot* are subsumed.

Rashi and Sa'adiah

In Exodus 24:12, we read:

> And the Lord said to Moses: "Come up to Me on the mountain and wait there; and I will give you the stone tablets, with the Torah and the Mitzvah that I have inscribed to instruct them."

Rashi's commentary discusses the phrase "the Torah and the Mitzvah" in its relationship to the tablets as if to ask: How can the

---

1. A literal translation would be "utterances," or, perhaps, "articles" (as in Articles of Confederation), but for the sake of clarity and consistency we shall continue to use the term Ten Commandments.

two stone tablets be so described when they contain only ten items? His answer is:

> All 613 *mitzvot* are contained in the Ten Commandments. And Rav Saʿadiah detailed, in the *Azharot* he composed, the *mitzvot* contained in each and every commandment.

What Are *Azharot*?

Azharot, to which Rashi referred, are a form of liturgical poetry (*piyyut*) that was reserved for poems composed for the *musaf* service of Shavuot enumerating the 613 Torah-prescribed commandments. One such poem was composed by Rabbi Saʿadiah Gaon (882–942), one of the most outstanding halakhists, exegetes, philosophers, and philologists of the Middle Ages.

The complete text of these *azharot* (the word literally means "cautions") is still recited on Shavuot by some Mizrachi (Oriental) Jewish communities (e.g., Yemenite, Syrian). Other Sephardic communities, such as the Spanish and Portuguese congregations, recite the *azharot* of another outstanding poet-philosopher, R. Solomon ibn Gabirol.

Here is the opening stanza of Saʿadiah's *Azharot*:[2]

> A blazing fire
> Brighter than the most brilliant light;
> And my words are like fire.
> In its sparks, there are many *mitzvot*
> Scintillating in each utterance.
> With wisdom, I gathered
> In my ten utterances
> Six hundred thirteen *mitzvot*,
> Demonstrating that the Lord's expressions
> Are made in purity.

---

2. Simcha Assaf and Israel Davidson (eds.): *Siddur Rav Saʿadiah Gaon* (Jerusalem, 1970), 191.

Sa'adiah then proceeded, in rhymed Hebrew verse,[3] to match every one of the 613 *mitzvot* to one or another of the Ten Commandments according to their sequence on the tablets:

Statement	# of *mitzvot*	Examples
Anokhi (I am the Lord your God)	80	*tzitzit, tefillin, mezuzah, tefillah, korbanot*
Lo yihyeh (have no other deities)	60	*molekh, kishuf, tum'at meit, nisu'ei ta'arovet*
Lo tissa (sacilege)	48	*dinim, hakhel, bal tosif, sin'at chinam, tokhechah*
Zakhor (remember the Sabbath)	75	*shalosh regalim, shemitah, yoveil, 'arei haleviyim*
Kabbed (honor your parents)	77	*milah, pidyon ha-ben, shilu'ach ha-ken, melukhah*
Lo tirtzach (murder)	50	*nezikin, ketoret zarah, navi sheker, ma'akeh, bal tashchit, ir ha-ni-dachat, goneiv nefesh*
Lo tin'af (adultery)	58	*sotah, yibbum ve-chalitzah, geirushin, keli gever, chupah ve-kiddushin*
Lo tignov (robbery)	59	*sekhar sakhir, shemittat kesafim, moznei tzedek, terumot u-ma'asrot, hassagat gevul, hashavat aveidah*
Lo ta'aneh (false witness)	52	*derishah ve-chakirah, leshon hara', metzora ve-toharato*
Lo tachmod (coveting)	54	*kashrut, n'veilot u-t'reifot, oto ve-et beno, gid ha-nasheh, kil'ayim, nazir*

---

3. The rhymed Hebrew verse of the *Azharot*, typical of medieval *piyyut*, is unusually complex and abstruse and will challenge the linguistic skills and ingenuity of even the most erudite reader.

Objective and Purpose

The principal subject of this essay is *ta'amei ha-mitzvot*: evaluating *mitzvot* from the perspective of their philosophical purpose, along with their practical performance. A concurrent objective is to organize *mitzvot* according to logical categories, and to find adequate and appropriate verbal articulation for those organizing principles. As the Book of Proverbs puts it so eloquently: "Like golden apples in silver showpieces, so is a well-turned phrase" (25:11).

That is to say: Golden apples, like well-chosen words, are valuable in and of themselves. When they are said at a particularly propitious moment, however, they become even more valuable – set, as it were, in silver showpieces.

For a detailed, albeit incomplete, distribution of these mitzvot, go back to the preceding chart. Before doing so, however, you might want to use your own reasoning processes and consider to which of these Ten Commandments you would assign the remaining *mitzvot*. Several approaches can be taken in this regard:

A. THE DEDUCTIVE APPROACH

This approach requires drawing a specific conclusion from a general proposition, and it consists of: (a) defining the categories represented by each of the *diberot*,[4] and (b) identifying the additional *mitzvot* that belong in each category.

For instance:

1. *Anokhi*, the first article, can be defined as a public testimony of faith; a perpetual readiness to acknowledge God. Which other *mitzvot* have that goal?
2. *Lo yih'yeh lekha* is a stern admonition against idolatry or, if we look at it from another angle, a strenuous reinforcement of the uniqueness and exclusivity of monotheism. Which other *mitzvot* provide that reinforcement?

---

4. The singular form of *diberot* is *dibeir* (cf. Jer. 5:13, 9:7).

3. *Kabeid* confirms and secures the rights and prerogatives of parents, and – by extension – affirms the need to maintain useful hierarchical social structures (i.e., "authority"). Which other *mitzvot* address the just regulation of an ordered society?
4. *Lo tirtzach* can be extended from the prohibition against murder to all regulations with the goal of eliminating bloodshed or preventing unnecessary or unwarranted loss of life. Can you think of other *mitzvot* whose objective is to avert such destruction?
5. *Lo tin'af* forbids not only adultery, but all forms of public and even private lewdness.
6. *Lo tignov* encompasses all the safeguards of private property, perhaps along with the social and ritual obligations that the acquisition of private property imposes.
7. *Lo tachmod* can be extended to all *mitzvot* that attempt to impose a discipline upon the senses.

B. THE INDUCTIVE APPROACH

An alternate approach is inductive, or deriving the general proposition from individual examples, and it consists of: (a) providing a ready-made division of select *mitzvot* according to the *diberot* and (b) identifying the organizing principles, or categories, which govern the division.

For instance:

1. If we include *tefilin* and *korbanot* under *Anokhi*, what category does it represent?
2. What principle is represented by *lo tissa'* (sacrilege) if it includes *bal tosif* and *sin'at chinam*?
3. Why would *leshon hara'* be included in *lo ta'aneh* (false witness) rather than in *lo tissa*?

C. THE RHETORICAL APPROACH

Or, try to relate select *mitzvot* to each of several categories, until you find the one to which you think it is particularly suited.

For instance:

1. Where would you include *keri'at Shema'*? In *Anokhi*? *Lo yih'yeh lekha*? Or, perhaps, in *Zakhor*?
2. Where do the following belong: *kashrut, yoveil, geneivat nefashot* (kidnapping), *terumot u-ma'asrot, keli gever,* or even *parah adumah*. (Note that according to rationalist Jewish philosophers, such as Maimonides, even the so-called *chukim* have rationales, although we may occasionally be unable to appreciate them.)

Whichever method you choose, or develop on your own, your objective remains – as described above – to stimulate the creative and reflective analysis of as many *mitzvot* or categories as possible.

Epilogue

The *aseret hadiberot* were originally included in the daily *shacharit* service. When early Christian anti-Jewish polemics (*tar'omet ha-minim*), seeking to curtail the legalistic nature of the Torah, found support in the exaggerated emphasis given to just these ten laws, the Sages deleted them from the daily liturgy. Moreover, in order to maintain their parity with other Torah commandments, they were denied any special recognition. Hence, Maimonides ruled (Responsa 263) that the congregation – if ordinarily seated for Torah readings – should not rise for their recitation as part of the weekly *sidrah*.

Wake Up and Smell the Torah! Coffee and the *Tikun Leil Shavuʻot*

Preface
Two practices long associated with Shavuot as "the time of the revelation of our Law" (*zeman matan Torateinu*) are the induction of children into religious school and the marathon all-night study vigil (*tikkun leil Shavuot*). The former is a venerable practice that appeared full-blown when first attested to in the literature of the German Pietists (*Chasidei Ashkenaz*) in the twelfth century, and has been the subject of serious scholarly analysis.[1] The latter is of considerably more recent vintage and will be the focus of our attention here.

The Tikun
R. Moses b. Judah Ibn Machir (Safed, 16th century), who provided our earliest notice of *Tikun Leil Shavuot*, attributed it to the Zohar's stipulation that it behooves anyone who dwells in the "royal palace" (i.e., the righteous) to engage in Torah study throughout the night of Shavuot. R. Isaiah ha-Levi Horowitz (Prague, 1560–1630),[2] who offered the earliest curriculum for that nocturnal vigil, attributed the *tikkun* to R. Shlomo ha-Levi Alkabetz, (author of the Friday night

---

1. See Ivan Marcus: *Rituals of Childhood* (Yale, 1996).
2. He is known as the *Shelah* after the acronym of his magnum opus *Sh'nei Luchot ha-B'rit*, "The Two Tablets of the Covenant," a singularly apt title in this holiday's context.

hymn *Lekhah Dodi*), a member of the "court" of the seminal Kabbalist R. Isaac Luria, and to his brother-in-law, R. Joseph Karo (author of the *Shulchan Arukh*).

While the origin of the Shavuot Tikun (and its antecedent, the daily midnight *tikun chatzot*) lies within the arcane mystical tradition, its feasibility and its popularity may have relied on a more mundane feature of early modern Jewish life: coffee.

Coffee

The earliest use of coffee is reported among the Sufis (Muslim mystics) of fifteenth-century Yemen who depended on it to keep them awake during their nighttime devotions. By the mid-16th century, its use had spread throughout the Middle East and coffeehouses arose to facilitate its consumption for secular as well as religious purposes. By the 18th century, it had become an exotic fixture – along with tea and sugar – of, initially, the upper-class and, later, the middle and lower classes in Central Europe, and a serious source of income for those who oversaw its preparation or distributed it.

In "Coffee, Coffeehouses and the Nocturnal Rituals of Early Modern Jewry,"[3] Elliot Horowitz, to whose thoroughly original insight this essay is indebted, wrote: "Where coffee spread, it extended the range of possibilities for making use of the night hours, whether for purposes pious or profane." More recently, Robert Liberles has added considerably to our understanding of the role that the importation, sale, and preparation of coffee had on German Jewry during the 18th century.[4]

Hilkhot Kofi

In Jewish communities, the preparation and use of coffee was distinguished by a characteristic consideration: *Halakhah*. Drinking

---

3. *AJS Review* 14 (1989).
4. *Jews Welcome Coffee* (Brandeis, 2012).

coffee raised such questions as Gentile cooking (*bishul akum*, or *bishulei nokhrim*). Sixteenth-century religious adjudicators (*poskim*) generally ruled that coffee made by non-Jews was "kosher" because it was made in utensils used exclusively for its preparation; they were uncomfortable, though, with its public consumption in coffeehouses, which appear to have been places of generally ill repute. Liberles took note of the fact that in dealing with coffee, Ashkenazi rabbis were wont to defer to the opinions of their Sephardi colleagues in the Ottoman Empire whose experience with the Oriental beverage was greater than their own.

After passing the bar of ritual law in general, the addictive nature of coffee created a singular problem that Liberles labeled "Shabbos coffee": the attempt to make hot coffee available on the Sabbath despite its complicated culinary laws. Here, as he demonstrated, such authorities as Jacob Emden (Altona, 1697–1776) and Ezekiel Landau (Prague, 1713–1793) displayed a marked inclination towards leniency by positing that the enhanced enjoyment of the Sabbath due to the consumption of coffee offset the largely technical concern over whether its brewing involved "secondhand cooking" (*bishul achar bishul*) – a dilemma long since ameliorated by the introduction of instant coffee.

Coffee and Shavuot

To illustrate the awareness within the halakhic community of the effects of caffeine and its application to the midnight vigil, Horowitz cited a 1673 responsum by R. Moses Zacuto of Italy, who was asked a mundane question about the prohibition against eating or drinking before morning prayers. After distinguishing between beverages such as wine and beer, which were prohibited, and water and medicines, which were permissible, he took cognizance of coffee's stimulant properties, and stated:

> We may cite as proof the custom throughout the land of Israel and the kingdom of Turkey where they are accustomed to drink

coffee [*qawi*] after every midnight, for it resembles a medicine that drives away sleep, as is well-known.

Tikun chatzot and coffee, then, both spread westward from Safed and Palestine across North Africa and into southern Europe during the sixteenth and seventeenth centuries, acquiring considerable popularity among Jews. The question is whether they were interrelated or just coincidental. Horowitz admitted that claiming coffee as the sole or even primary stimulus for the institution of the midnight *tikun* would be "reductionist." Nevertheless, he asserted:

> The introduction of coffee brought with it, beyond the mere availability of a new stimulant, the emergence of a new perception of the night in which the hours of darkness could be shaped and manipulated by human initiative rather than condemn man to passive repose.

A Sip to Be Sociable

But drinking coffee became more than that. It acquired an independent standing as a mark of closure for both business dealings and social affairs, akin to the status enjoyed today by a champagne toast. Liberles, reflecting on this development, concluded:

> It is possible that the role of coffee went beyond its caffeine content. I would suggest that by incorporating coffee into the very protocol of the ritual, it was transformed into a sacred version of the secular coffee gathering. In short, coffee continually proves itself quite a versatile performer, and in that sense it is ideal to fill multiple functions, from the secular to the more sacredly enhanced.

The World in Suspended Animation
Matan Torah in Aggadah

Preface

A characteristic theme struck by the Aggadah is that the entire universe was created solely for the Torah. This manifests itself in such well-known statements as "God looked into the Torah and created the world" (Zohar, *Terumah*) or in the homily that interprets the Torah's first word, *Bereishit*, as "for the sake of Torah, which is called *reishit*" (*Lekach Tov*, *Bereishit* 1). The converse, as we shall see, is also true: Without Torah, existence is endangered.

Existence Depends on Torah

According to several *aggadot*, if the observance of Torah were to cease, the world would return to the chaotic state whence it originally emerged.

1. The Talmud (*Shabbat* 88a) states:

    God stipulated a condition with the outcomes of creation: If Israel accepts the Torah, you will be sustained. If not, I shall restore you to chaos and void.

2. And elsewhere (*Pesachim* 68b), we find:

    "Thus said the Lord. If not for my covenant, day and night, I would not have established the limits of heaven and earth" (Jeremiah 33:25). If not for Torah, heaven and earth would not be sustained.

This idea is also reflected in the classic commentary of Rashi in the very first chapter of the Torah:

3. On Genesis 1:31: "There was sunset and sunrise: The sixth day" (*va-y'hi 'erev va-y'hi boker, yom ha-shishi*), Rashi stipulated:

   [The Torah] added the [definite article] *heih* to the sixth day[1] at the conclusion of the act of creation, to indicate that [God] imposed a condition on it: [namely] that Israel accepts the five books of the Torah.[2]

4. Rashi then adds an alternative explanation of *ha-shishi*:

   All [creation] was kept in suspension (*teluyim ve'om'dim*) until the sixth day of Sivan, which was prepared for the delivery of the Torah.

According to this alternate interpretation, "the sixth" is an allusion to the calendar date of Shavuot, the traditional anniversary of the giving of the Torah (*matan Torah*).

Nature Awaited Torah Expectantly

An outgrowth of the previous idea is conveyed in several beautiful *aggadot* that depict elements of nature participating in the drama of the giving of the Torah, as though they recognized that their own existence depended upon it.

1. *Exodus Rabbah* (29:9): A rivalry developed among the mountains as to where *matan Torah* should occur.

   When God came to deliver the Torah at Sinai, Mount Tabor and Mount Carmel began running about and arguing with one another. One said: "The Torah will be delivered on

---

1. The five previous days are grammatically indefinite (*echad, sheini, shelishi*, etc.) while it is *"the"* sixth day, using the definite article.
2. The alpha-numerical value of the letter *heih* is five.

me," while the other said: "The Torah will be delivered on me."

As we know, the Torah was delivered on neither of those two mountains (arguably, the most prominent mountains in the Land of Israel), but upon Mt. Sinai, a mountain so inconspicuous[3] that its very location is uncertain.

2. Also in *Exodus Rabbah* (29:9):

> When God delivered the Torah, birds neither chirped nor flew, oxen did not bellow, the sea was tranquil, and people did not speak. The entire world waited in silence until the voice [*kol*] was heard saying: "I am the Lord your God."

The sense of anticipation fraught with anxiety is almost palpable in these depictions.

Har KeGigit: Giving Torah by Force?

The aggadic narrative of *matan Torah* contains a problematic passage whose interpretation has long divided sages and scholars. *Shabbat* 88a (the *locus classicus* of this subject), which we have cited above, states:

> "They stood at the bottom of the mountain" (Exodus 19:17): R. Avdimi ben Hasa said: This teaches us that God overturned the mountain above them as though it were a barrel, saying to them: If you accept the Torah, well and good, but if not, there you shall be buried.

The normative interpretation of this passage follows the subsequent remarks of R. Aha bar Yaakov: "This clearly constitutes grounds for the denial of responsibility for the Torah" (*moda'a rabbah le'oraita'*). As

---

3. Later sources portray Mt. Sinai as a paragon of humility. Cf. R. Isaiah Horowitz: *Sh'nei Luchot ha-B'rit* (*Sha'ar ha-'Otiyot: 'Anavah*).

explained by Rashi: "If God were to sue Israel for breach of promise, they could reply: We received the Torah under duress." Indeed, the Talmud, in the continuation, argues that the binding legal force of Torah observance is not due to its original forcible acceptance at Sinai, as much as its subsequent voluntary acceptance at the time of Purim. At that time, despite the incentive to renounce their distinctive laws and practices, the Jews chose to "uphold and cherish" their traditions (Esther 9:27), in perpetuity.

An Alternate Reading

Yitzhak Heinemann, one of the foremost modern interpreters of Aggadah, offered an alternate scenario. He suggested that R. Aha, with a Babylonian's typical preoccupation with juridical affairs, may have grossly misunderstood the intent of the Palestinian R. Avdimi, who was speaking in the highly symbolic aggadic mode, more typical of the Land of Israel.

In light of the preceding sources surrounding the equation between Torah and sustained existence, we may understand Avdimi to have meant that since the world was dependent on the acceptance of the Torah, God was advising Israel that its rejection of the Torah would mean the end of the world: "There you shall be buried" because everything would revert to utter nihility (*tohu va-vohu*).

Indeed, Heinemann's interpretation is consistent with yet another legend surrounding *matan Torah*, namely that God offered the Torah to other nations – who declined it.

First of all, God approached the descendants of Esau[4] and said to them: "Will you accept the Torah?" They replied: "Master of

---

4. In talmudic lore, this is a standard designation first for Romans and, later, for Christians. See Moshe Sokolow: "Esav; From Edom to Rome," in Daniel Z. Feldman, Stuart W. Halperin (eds.): *Mitokh Ha-Ohel; Essays on the Weekly Haftarah Reading from the Rabbis and Professors of Yeshiva University* (NY: Yeshiva University Press, 2011), 65–77.

the Universe; what is written in it?" He said: "Do not murder."
They replied: "Our entire essence is based upon bloodshed
[*cherev*], as our ancestor [Isaac] promised [his son Esau]: 'You
shall live by the sword' (Genesis 27:40). We cannot accept the
Torah."

He went next to the descendants of Ishmael[5] and said: "Will
you accept the Torah?" They replied... (*Pesikta Rabbati* 21).

Because God had already been turned down by the other nations of
the world, Israel was the last resort. If they, too, had declined to accept
the Torah, the word would have lost its *raison d'etre* and everything –
not Israel alone – would have reverted to chaos and void.

Halakhah and Aggadah: Creative Tension

The tension between jurisprudence and folklore hinted at in Heinemann's explanation of the misunderstanding between R. Aha and R. Avdimi, and the common preference for the latter over the former is captured by the following Aggadah:

> R. Abbahu and R. Hiyya b. Abba once came to a place. R.
> Abbahu expounded Aggadah and R. Hiyya b. Abba expounded
> legal matters (*shema'ata*).[6] All the people left R. Hiyya b. Abba
> and went to hear R. Abbahu, so that the former was upset.
>
> [R. Abbahu] said to him: "I will give you a parable. To
> what is the matter like? To two men, one of whom was selling
> precious stones and the other various kinds of small ware. To
> whom will the people hurry? Is it not to the seller of various
> kinds of small ware?" (*Sotah* 40a).

---

5. Arabs; later Muslims. The redaction of *Pesikta Rabbati* is generally dated to the ninth century.
6. Literally: "something heard." It is an allusion to the originally oral nature of the Jewish legal tradition and is a meaningful counterpart to the term *aggadah* (or *haggadah*), which literally means something told over.

Hayyim Nahman Bialik (1873–1934), who studied at the Volozhin yeshiva as a young man, captured the essence of this tension in an essay entitled "Halakhah and Aggadah," that often appears as the prologue to *Sefer ha-Aggadah*, an anthology he published. His précis is:

> The face of *halakhah* is stern, while that of *aggadah* is merry. The former is exacting, strict and tough as nails; the attribute of justice (*middat ha-din*). The latter is forgiving, lenient, as soothing as oil; the attribute of compassion (*middat ha-rachamim*).

Rabbi A.I. Kook (1865–1935), likewise an alumnus of Volozhin, proposed the following reconciliation:

> We must stress the joining of these two forces in a proper form, so that each will give added strength to the content of the other, help clarify its particulars and shed more light on its general concepts, on the depth of its logic and its far-reaching significance.
>
> The *halakhah* must be made more appealing through association with the *aggadah*, in an appropriate manner, and the *aggadah*, likewise, needs to be assessed in its relationship to the clearly defined fixed laws and the particularized delimiting logic represented in the established structure of the *halakhah*. Thereby will the vitality and fruitfulness of both be doubled.[7]

---

7. Rabbi Abraham Isaac Kook: "The Unification of Halakhah and Aggada," *The Lights of Holiness* I, 25–28.

Sheyibaneh Beit Hamikdash
Rebuilding the Temple: Rav Kook, Rabbi Hayyim Hirschensohn, and Theodor Herzl

Preface

At the conclusion of every *'Amidah*, we recite the following passage:

> May it be Your will, Lord our God and God of our ancestors, that the Temple will be rebuilt speedily in our times. May we merit a share in Your Torah. There we shall serve You reverentially as in days of yore and years gone by.

Among the medievals, only Maimonides took this practically enough to incorporate a section entitled "The Laws of the Temple" into his *Mishneh Torah*; otherwise, it was consigned to a purely theoretical dimension of *halakhah* known, conventionally, as "Laws for the Messianic Age" (*hilkheta' di-meshicha'*). With the gathering strength of the Zionist movement in the late 19th century, and, even more so, with the issuing of the Balfour Declaration in 1917, the "Messianic Age" suddenly appeared to be closer than anticipated, prompting renewed speculation over the rebuilding of the Temple and renewal of animal sacrifices.

Here we shall compare three approaches to these issues: those of Rabbi Abraham Isaac HaKohen Kook (1865–1935), who served as Chief Ashkenazic Rabbi of Mandatory Palestine, Rabbi Hayyim

Hirschensohn (1857–1935), Chief Rabbi of Hoboken, New Jersey, and Theodor Herzl, father of modern political Zionism.[1]

Rav Kook

In 1918, Menasheh Grossberg, a Russian-born rabbi living in London, sent a letter to Rav Kook who was residing in London at that time (due to World War I, he could not return to Palestine), asking, inter alia, whether it was permissible to rebuild the Temple, even if no sacrifices would be offered. Rav Kook's reply split a halakhic hair. Based on Maimonides's stipulation that the purpose in rebuilding the Temple was to renew the sacrificial order, he denied that it would fulfill a mitzvah, but allowed that rebuilding it, per se, even without sacrifices, was permissible.

> In any event, to the best of my knowledge, if it will be God's will that we will rebuild the Temple even before the Messiah comes and prophecy is renewed and wonders will be observed, there will be no impediment in this matter. However, the mitzvah is to build the Temple in order to sacrifice there, and to celebrate the festivals whose essence is also the offering of the festive sacrifices. However, to say that if sacrifices are not offered is a transgression of "do not act thus with me" (Exodus 20:20) by building a purposeless building, is not at all reasonable. Rather, it is the performance of an incomplete mitzvah to build a temple and not offer sacrifices, if they are available. (*Mishpat Kohen* 179–180)

Some three years later, Rav Kook took a more conservative position, writing a longer and more detailed halakhic monograph entitled

---

[1]. This chapter owes a debt of gratitude to Eyal ben Eliyahu: "To Build a New Sanctuary?: Rabbi Kook, Rabbi Hirschensohn, and Theodor Herzl on the Rebuilding of the Temple and Renewal of Sacrifices," *Cathedra* 128 (Summer, 2008), 101–112. The translations, interpretations, and applications, however, are mine.

"The Contemporary Sanctity of the Temple Site," which deals with access to the Temple area, an obvious precondition for its rebuilding. Central to his argument are a ruling of Maimonides prohibiting entry (*Hilkhot Beit ha-Bechirah* 6:14–15) and the contrary opinion of Rabbi Abraham ben David (Rabad; Provence 1120–1198), who reduced the infraction from a severe Torah prohibition to a less serious rabbinical one. Rav Kook wrote:

> In any event, there remains a contemporary prohibition even according to Raabad. Even if we were to say that Raabad came to say that, halakhically, this does not incur excision nowadays, we might yet say that there remains [the transgression of] both a prohibition and a positive commandment... It remains prohibited for a Jew because all consecrations remain in force, along with their accompanying prohibitions.... The Temple will speedily be built in our day in all its glory and splendor and sanctity when He dispatches to us Elijah the prophet to notify us of the impending redemption. (*Mishpat Kohen* 218)

The reversal between 1918 and 1921 in his attitude towards the rebuilding may have resulted from his appointment, in the interim, as Chief Ashkenazic Rabbi of Mandatory Palestine, a responsibility that may have motivated him to adopt a more conservative public posture. (It has been noted that he similarly retreated from earlier positions on the renewal of *semikhah* and the Sanhedrin.)

Rabbi Hirschensohn

Hayyim Hirschensohn was born in Safed in 1857 to a family that had joined the *Chibat Tziyon* (Love of Zion) movement and educated in a yeshiva named for Rabbi Eliyahu Guttmacher, one of the forerunners of religious Zionism. Active in political and cultural affairs, he shared with Eliezer ben Yehudah the ambition of reviving the Hebrew language and raised his own children in it. As a Mizrachi (Religious Zionist) delegate to the 6th Zionist Congress in 1903, he broke ranks with the movement and opposed the Uganda plan. Later that year, he immigrated to the United States and assumed the post of Chief Rabbi of Hoboken, NJ, a position that he felt (correctly) would allow him adequate leisure for study and publication. He remained in Hoboken until his death in 1935.

When the Balfour Declaration was issued in November of 1917, Hirschensohn was elated at the prospect of the renewal of Jewish sovereignty over the Land of Israel. He proceeded to devote his prodigious intellectual energies and his vast erudition in both Jewish and secular sources to formulating halakhic guidelines for the merger of his two most central causes: the Jewish tradition, to which he had been committed from birth, and the American tradition of democracy, under whose spell he had fallen since his arrival in the United States. His efforts resulted in the publication of *Malki BaKodesh*, six volumes of responsa (in Hebrew) devoted to the clarification of such issues as the rights of women, non-Orthodox Jews, non-Jews, etc.[2]

The first two responsa deal with the questions of monarchy and sacrifices, respectively. In the former case, he ruled that monarchy had been replaced by democracy (*memshelet 'am*):

> How can we anticipate the arrival of the Messiah in order to appoint a king who will rule, along with his descendants, forever, since the entire world, and the Jewish people, a singularly wise and understanding nation, all know and recognize that the time of democracy has come, that the rule of one man over a nation is over.

And in the case of sacrifices, he wrote:

> Everyone shall understand that God is not satisfied with the fat of sheep or libations of oil. If Israel, as a nation [in the past], practiced sacrifices, and even if a flame descended from

---

2. This work was popularized by Eliezer Schweid in *Democracy and Halakhah* (Lanham: University Press, 1994).

heaven to consume the sacrifices, that is on account of a deep hidden secret kept in God's storehouse, that we are unable to comprehend (*Malki BaKodesh* vol. 1, St. Louis, 1919; 8 ff.).

The third responsum, entitled "Entry to the Temple Site," proposed building a Temple to be called "The Palace of Peace" (*Heikhal HaShalom*), a term borrowed from Herzl (see below), that was to be a universal spiritual center, devoid of sacrifice.

> This place must be sacred for song and poetry and prayers to God, Who chooses amongst the melodious poems beyond all matter of song and praise of David the sweet singer of Israel, and of our contemporary poets, to offer sacred poems. All the scholars of Israel will preach from there to the people about righteousness and law and ethics. There will be the courts of justice, the Supreme Court of Jerusalem, from which Torah and light will emanate throughout the world. This house will be a House of Prayer for all nations. There will not be any statues or symbols particular to any single nation; only the two tablets of the covenant that are the pillars of all civilization... (Ibid., 11–12).

Binyamin Ze'ev (Theodor) Herzl

In Chapter 5 of *Altneuland*, a novel about life in a utopian Jewish homeland, Herzl described his rebuilt Temple.

> They reached the temple. The times had fulfilled themselves, and it was rebuilt. Once more it had been erected with great quadrangular blocks of stone hewn from nearby quarries and hardened by the action of the atmosphere. Once more the pillars of bronze stood before the holy place of Israel. "The left pillar was called Boaz, but the name of the right was Jachin." In the forecourt was a mighty bronze altar, with an enormous basin called the Brazen Sea as in the olden days when Solomon was king in Israel.

The Great Hall resounded with singing and the playing of lutes. The music recalled to Frederick [Herzl's hero] far off things in his own life and turned his thoughts to other days in Israel. The worshippers were crooning and murmuring the words of the ritual, but Frederick thought of Heine's Hebrew melodies. The Princess Sabbath, she that is called the serene Princess, was at home here. The choristers chanted a hymn that had stirred yearnings for their own land for hundreds of years. The words of the noble poet Solomon haLevy: "Lecha Dodi likrat kallah – Come beloved to meet the bride."

Suddenly, as Friedrich listened to the music and meditated on the thoughts it inspired, the significance of the Temple flashed upon him. In the days of King Solomon, it had been a gorgeous symbol, adorned with gold and precious stones, attesting to the might and the pride of Israel... Yet, however splendid it might have been, the Jew could not have grieved it for eighteen centuries long... No, they sighed for an invisible something of which the stones had been a symbol. It had come to rest in the rebuilt Temple, where stood the home-returning sons of Israel who lifted up their souls to the invisible God as their fathers had done on Mount Moriah. The words of Solomon glowed with new vitality: "The Lord hath said that he would dwell in the thick darkness/ I have surely built Thee a house of habitation/A place for Thee to dwell in forever."[3]

The allusion to the incorporation into the rebuilt Temple of stones that came from the same source as one of its predecessors is testimony to Herzl's acquaintance with Central European Jewish folklore. As one historian wrote:

In fact, Herzl's familiarity with the symbolism and mythology of the Temple stones seems to have been quite sophisticated.

---

3. Theodor Herzl: *Altneuland, The Old-New Land* (Wildside Press, 2018), 253 ff.

The title of the book itself, Altneuland, was explicitly borrowed from the German name of the medieval synagogue of Prague, the Altneushul. One classic story of the Altneushul describes the origins of the shul's cornerstone as being a stone from the destroyed Temple, carried into exile and used to construct the synagogue. With the coming of the Messiah, the story goes, the stone would be miraculously transported back to Jerusalem to take its place in the rebuilt Temple.[4]

The overall impression of Herzl's Temple, however, struck one of his leading adversaries, Achad Ha`Am, as more akin to the Reform Temple Herzl was familiar with in Vienna. In his review and critique of *Altneuland*, he wrote of Herzl's Jerusalem:

> In general, the old city has changed little. The ancient prayer houses of all the religions still stand in place; even the Muslim mosque named for Omar still stands on the Temple Mount as before. But new public buildings have been added to the old, outstanding among them is the "Palace of Peace" (*Heikhal HaShalom*) from which assistance goes out to the entire world to deal with any tragedy occurring anywhere. A council composed of the various religions oversees the division of the space, ensuring it is right and proper. On the gates of the palace is inscribed the well-known Roman proverb: "Nothing human is alien to me."
>
> Among the new buildings of the old city, the Temple will arise splendidly. Yes, the Temple; with the "Yakhin and Boaz columns," "Solomon's pool," and with an altar in its courtyard. Why an altar? We cannot know, because not a word is mentioned in the book about sacrifices. All we know is that on the Sabbath eve a chorus sings L'kha Dodi to musical

---

4. Steven Fine: *The Temple of Jerusalem: From Moses to the Messiah*: In Honor of Professor Louis H. Feldman. Brill, 2011.

accompaniment – just like in the "Temple" in Vienna; no more.

And why an altar? But if we come to ask, there is an even more serious question. Where shall the Temple be built? As we have noted, the Mosque of Omar still stands on the site of the Chosen Edifice (*beit ha-bechirah*); did Rabbi Shmuel, friend to the Liberals, permit the Temple to be built elsewhere?

However, one may not question Altneuland, which is entirely miraculous.[5]

Rav Kook's Reaction to Hirschensohn

Hirschensohn, as was his wont, circulated his work widely and invited responses, which he published. Rav Kook, while agreeing with his position on democracy – at least tentatively – took sharp issue with his view on the Temple and sacrifice. Hirschensohn published Rav Kook's response in a later volume of his responsa. Here, Rav Kook, too, testifies to Herzl's influence.

> However, regarding the site of the Temple, my opinion [i.e., Rav Kook] is quite distant from yours [Hirschensohn] ... It makes more sense to say that even according to the Raabad there is a Torah prohibition ... or at the very least a rabbinical prohibition, and we cannot allow masses of impure people to approach the site of the glorious throne, the elevated site of our Temple ... In my opinion it would be more respectful if we would acquire possession of the courtyards adjacent to the holy Kotel and on that site, in proximity to the Kotel, build a

---

5. *Kol Kitvei Achad Ha'Am*, 319. Translation based on the Hebrew text appearing on https://benyehuda.org/read/5527#fn:50. Rabbi Shmuel, the religious persona of the utopian novel, is presumed to be patterned after Rabbi Shmuel Mohliver (1824–1898), an early supporter of the Hibat Tziyon movement. By "miraculous" (*ma'aseh nissim*) in the closing sentence, I assume Achad Ha`am meant something closer to fictitious.

great and glorious synagogue. And all those innovations that you have recommended, for song and religious poetry, will be conducted there... This is consistent with the vision of Herzl in *Altneuland* about the Temple, even if it does not stand literally on the site of the Temple... (*Malki baKodesh* vol. 4, St. Louis, 1922, 4 ff.)

Hirschensohn appended a retort of his own calling Rav Kook's suggestion about a palatial synagogue adjacent to the Kotel disingenuous, and comparable to the Uganda Plan (which, as we noted, Hirschensohn had opposed).

[Regarding] Your idea to build a minor temple not on its real location but west of the Western Wall... The hearts of Israel are tied to that site and through it to their Father in heaven. However, that will not heal the wounds of our hearts as long as we cannot ascend the Temple Mount itself. This resembles the Uganda plan offered prior to our acquisition of our ancestral homeland. However, whenever the site of the temple will be sanctified, we may add that adjacent site to it as prophesied by Ezekiel... (*Malki baKodesh* 4, 8)

Restoration of Sacrifices

As far as sacrifices are concerned, Rav Kook, in his response to Hirschensohn, had written:

Regarding sacrifices, it would be more proper to believe that everything will return to its previous status and that and we will no longer be influenced by the philosophies of European civilization... It is unworthy of us to imagine that sacrifices rest entirely on the base idea of anthropomorphic worship... But I agree with you that we cannot approach the matter of sacrifices without the appearance of the Holy Spirit; something that is in itself not a very distant or unimaginable expectation because the Lord can appear suddenly... (*Malki ba-Kodesh* vol. 4, St. Louis, 1922, 4 ff.)

However, in his commentary to the Siddur, expressed an alternate idea more consistent with his acknowledged advocacy of vegetarianism:

> Animals that are offered on the altar are elevated by virtue of being sacrificed to God because they possess no intellect and can achieve this elevation only when acted upon in the form of sacrifice. Humans, however, who can understand the act of sacrifice, can approach God intellectually. In the future, knowledge will spread and be refined even amongst animals... and the manner of sacrifice then will be that of meal offerings, made from vegetation, that will yet be as pleasing to God as in days of yore and years gone by.[6]

---

6. *Olat Re'iyah* (Jerusalem, 1938), 296.